# GCSE Modern World History

Allan Todd

Series Editor: Jayne de Courcy

# Contents

Published by HarperCollins*Publishers* Ltd
77–85 Fulham Palace Road
London W6 8JB





First published 2001

ISBN 0 00 710976 8



British Library Cataloguing in Publication Data
A catalogue record for this book is available from the British Library

Edited by Kate Woodhouse
Production by Kathryn Botterill
Design by Gecko Limited
Cover design by Susi Martin-Taylor
Printed and bound by Scotprint Ltd., Haddington

**Acknowledgements**
The Author and Publishers are grateful to the following for permission to reproduce copyright material:

**Photographs**
Camera Press 88, 92
Hulton Getty Images 9, 14, 18, 29, 98, 105
Imperial War Museum 5, 8, 23, 35, 82
David King 37, 45, 47, 51, 55, 57, 58
Peter Newark's Pictures 63, 71
Popperfoto 32
Süddeutscher Verlag 25
Topham Picturepoint 65, 68, 69

**Illustrations**
Gecko Ltd 2, 4, 73, 80, 116
Jillian Luff 16, 44, 106
Julia Osorno 103



Every effort has been made to contact the holders of copyright material, but if any have been inadvertently overlooked, the Publishers will be pleased to make the necessary arrangements at the first opportunity.

# Get the most out of your Instant Revision pocket book

1. **Maximise your revision time.** You can carry this book around with you anywhere. This means you can spend any spare moments dipping into it.
2. **Learn and remember what you need to know.** This book contains all the really important things you need to know for your exam. All the information is set out clearly and concisely, making it easy for you to revise.
3. **Find out what you don't know.** The *Check yourself* questions and *Score chart* help you to see quickly and easily the topics you're good at and those you're not so good at.

## What's in this book?

### 1 The facts – just what you need to know

- There are sections for all the core Modern World History topics set by all the Exam Boards.
- The information is laid out in short blocks so that it is easy to read and remember.

### 2 *Check yourself* questions – find out how much you know and boost your grade

- Each *Check yourself* is linked to one or more facts page. The numbers after the topic heading in the *Check yourself* tell you which facts page the *Check yourself* is linked to.

- The questions are quick to answer. They aren't actual exam questions but they will show you what you do and don't know.
- The reverse side of each *Check yourself* gives you the answers **plus** tutorial help and guidance to boost your exam grade.
- There are points for each question. The total number of points for each *Check yourself* is always 20. When you check your answers, fill in the score box alongside each answer with the number of points you feel you scored.

## 3 The *Score chart* – an instant picture of your strengths and weaknesses

- *Score chart (1)* lists all the *Check yourself* pages.
- As you complete each *Check yourself*, record your points on the *Score chart*. This will show you instantly which areas you need to spend more time on.
- *Score chart (2)* is a graph which lets you plot your points against GCSE grades. This will give you a rough idea of how you are doing in each area. Of course, this is only a rough idea because the questions aren't real exam questions!

**Use this Instant Revision pocket book on your own – or revise with a friend or relative. See who can get the highest score!**

## The War begins

- The First World War began on 4 August 1914, when Britain declared war on Germany, after German armies had invaded Belgium.
- The years before had seen increasing international tension and an **arms race** between the most powerful European countries.
- These countries had formed two rival alliances:

| **The Allies** *(also known as the Triple Entente)* | **The Central Powers** *(also known as the Triple Alliance)* |
|---|---|
| Britain | Germany |
| France | Austria–Hungary |
| Russia | Italy (stayed neutral in 1914, then switched to the Allies in 1915) |
| | Turkey (joined in 1914). |

- German fears of facing a two-front war (with Russia in the east, France in the west) led its military planners to draw up the **Schlieffen Plan**. This was to knock France out quickly via Belgium, to avoid French defences, before the Russian army could be mobilised.
- But the Schlieffen Plan failed because:
  - the Belgian army's resistance slowed the German advance.
  - the Russian army had begun to mobilise (because of the Serbian dispute with Austria–Hungary).
  - Britain, worried by the invasion of Belgium, sent a small army (the British Expeditionary Force) to help France.
- After the Allies counter-attacked (Battle of the Marne), the exhausted Germans retreated to a line of trenches, after just failing to reach Paris.
- Both sides then tried to capture the Channel ports first in '**the rush – or race – to the sea**'. By November 1914, the system of trenches on the Western front stretched from the North Sea to Switzerland (470 km). It was clear that a short war ('**over by Christmas**') was extremely unlikely – especially as both sides were roughly equal in numbers and weapons.

## Stalemate on the Western Front

- By November 1914, both sides were dug into trenches along the Western Front, partly because new weapons, like **machine guns** and **heavy artillery**, were better suited to defence than attack.
- Opposing trenches were separated by **No Man's Land**, across which attacks took place ('**going over the top**').
- Life in the trenches was hard with **mud**, '**trench foot**', **lice**, **rats**.
- Generals on both sides tried unsuccessfully to break the **stalemate** by using new tactics and weapons: **heavy artillery barrages**, **gas attacks** from 1915, **tanks** from 1916.
- There were many major battles, for example, Ypres 1915, Verdun 1916, the Somme 1916, Passchendaele 1917.
- Though losses were heavy, very little ground was ever gained. The stalemate continued – it had become a '**war of attrition**'.

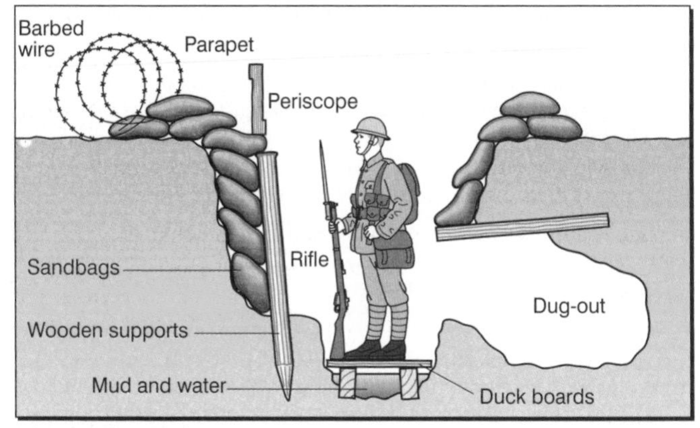


*Diagram of a trench*

# The War on other Fronts

## The Eastern Front

Fighting involved the Russians against Austria–Hungary and Germany.

- Early battles in 1914 (**Tannenberg**, August; the **Masurian Lakes**, September) led to heavy Russian losses, but there was no trench warfare as on the Western Front.
- A successful Russian counter-attack in June 1916, the **Brusilov Offensive**, was soon pushed back. Russian troops lacked weapons, supplies and good leaders. By the end of 1916, German troops occupied large areas of Russia and one million Russian soldiers had deserted.

## The Balkans

- The most important conflict was the **Gallipoli Campaign**, designed to capture the **Dardanelles** and so weaken Germany's ally, Turkey. But it was badly planned and the Turkish army defended well. After months of trench warfare, Allied forces withdrew in December 1915.
- The Allies also fought Bulgaria, which joined the Central Powers in 1915, along the **Salonika Front** in north Greece.

## The Italian Front

- Italy joined the Allies in 1915 attracted by promises of Austrian land after the war. She fought hard against Austro–Hungarian and German troops but suffered heavy losses at the **Battle of Caporetto, 1917**.

## The Middle East

- Vital **oil supplies** were threatened by Turkey, Germany's ally, which ruled much of the Middle East. British campaigns in **Mesopotamia** were unsuccessful, but in **Palestine** T E Lawrence helped stir up an Arab revolt against their Turkish rulers.

## East Africa

- The Allies captured all four German colonies, but the German commander in German East Africa conducted a guerrilla campaign until the end of the war.

## The war at sea

- Both Britain and Germany had large navies. As most European countries could not feed themselves, in a long war navies would be essential to protect **merchant fleets** bringing food supplies from overseas colonies.
- The surface fleets were equipped with '**Dreadnoughts**', the new battleships. They only fought one major battle, at **Jutland in 1916**.
- Submarines (**U-boats**) posed a more serious threat. From 1915, German U-boats attacked British merchant fleets in response to the **British blockade** of German ports.
- After April 1917 Britain adopted new counter-tactics. The **convoy system**, where large numbers of ships grouped together with an armed escort, was particularly effective.

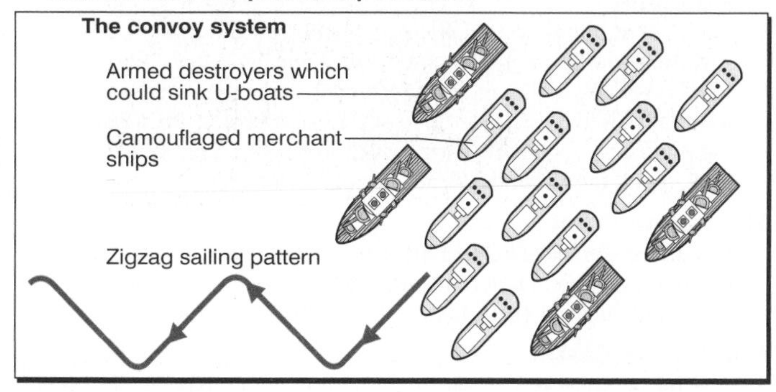


## The war in the air

- **Airships** (Zeppelins) were used by Germany to bomb British cities; but these had poor navigation, especially in bad weather. Improved British defences led to many being shot down.
- **Aeroplanes** were first used to observe and photograph (called **scouting**) enemy trenches. Later, they were fitted with fixed machine-guns, which led to the first air battles ('**dog fights**'). Bombers were also developed by both sides. At first, bombs were dropped by hand.

## The First World War (1–4)

1 Which country did Germany invade in August 1914, causing Britain to declare war? (1)

2 Name the German war plan which the German Commander von Moltke attempted to follow in August 1914. (1)

3 What was Britain's side in the First World War known as? (1)

4 On which side did Italy fight? (1)

5 Who were the 'contemptibles'? (1)

6 What was 'No Man's Land'? (1)

7 Apart from heavy artillery barrages, name *one* thing that made life in the trenches unpleasant. (1)

8 In which battle of 1916 were tanks first used? (1)

9 What gas was first used by the Germans in April 1915 during the second Battle of Ypres? (1)

10 By what other name is the 1917 Battle of Passchendaele known? (1)

11 Explain briefly what is meant by a 'war of attrition'. (2)

12 Write one or two sentences to explain the importance of the Eastern Front. (2)

13 Why were U-boats such a threat to Britain? (3)

14 How did Britain deal with this threat? (3)

# ANSWERS & TUTORIALS

SCORE

**1** Belgium. (1) In 1839, Britain had signed a treaty promising to guarantee Belgium's neutrality.
**2** The Schlieffen Plan. (1) Drawn up in 1895, it was intended to defeat France in six weeks so German troops would be free to fight Russia.
**3** The Allies (1) *or* Triple Entente. (1) The other two countries were France and Russia.
**4** Britain's. (1)

**5** The BEF or British Expeditionary Force. (1)
**6** The land between the two front lines on the Western Front controlled by neither side. (1)

**7** Any *one* from: mud *or* frostbite *or* lice *or* rats *or* poor food. (1)

**8** The Somme. (1) They were used towards the end of the battle. Their first serious use was the Battle of Cambrai, 1917.
**9** Chlorine. (1) Phosgene and mustard gas were also used by both sides, but they were less reliable.
**10** Third Battle of Ypres. (1) There were 500,000 British casualties for a gain of 8 kilometres.
**11** To defeat an enemy by destroying more of their forces than they do of yours. (1) This led to heavy casualties on both sides in the First World War. (1)
**12** It forced the Germans to divert troops from the Western Front which relieved pressure on British and French forces. (1) Russia's invasion of Germany in 1914 forced von Moltke to move 100,000 troops to the east which contributed to the failure of the Schlieffen Plan. (1)
**13** Britain needed to import food to survive. (1) By April 1917, 25 per cent of British merchant shipping was being destroyed by U-boats. (1) If this had continued, Britain might have faced serious food shortages and so been unable to continue to fight. (1)
**14** It introduced the convoy system in 1917. (1) Merchant ships sailed in zig-zag patterns protected by destroyers (1) It developed hydrophones to detect submarines. (1)

TOTAL

## The Home Front: the government

- Once it became clear that it would not be a short war, **Lord Kitchener** drew up plans to recruit a large army:
  - 1914–15: government propaganda persuaded a million **volunteers** to join up. Promises were made to keep volunteers from the same area or factory together (**Pals Regiments**).
  - 1916: by January news of the massive casualties and bad conditions on the Western Front meant there were fewer volunteers. So, the government passed a law to force **conscription** (compulsory military service) on all single men aged 18–41; later in 1916, this was extended to married men.
  - 1918: the age for conscription was raised to 50.
- The government exempted some men from conscription:
  - those in **reserved occupations** (essential jobs) – miners, skilled factory workers, farmers.
  - the medically unfit.
  - **conscientious objectors**: COs or 'conchies', people who were morally opposed to war. Tribunals decided which people were genuine. At first, many were forced into the army but later they were put in prison.
- The government also passed the **Defence of the Realm Act (DORA)**, which gave it the powers to:
  - **take over** the running of factories, mines and land.
  - **censor** (control) the war news to decide what reached the people and to keep journalists away from the Front. At first, only victories were reported, and details of losses were released in stages. Censorship became more difficult as casualties rose.
- The government used **propaganda** to:
  - persuade men to volunteer.
  - make people hate the Germans
  - keep up the morale of people at home
  - persuade everyone to play a part in the war effort.

# THE FIRST WORLD WAR (6)

- The First World War was Britain's first **total war**. The government soon realised that everyone would be involved, especially **women**.
- By 1915, it was clear that a large army and a long war meant that women would have to keep industry going as:
  - factory workers
  - tram drivers, ticket inspectors
  - secretaries and clerks
  - workers in **munitions** factories making weapons and shells (by 1918 there were over 900,000 'munitionettes')
  - farm workers in the **Women's Land Army**.
- Most women supported the war from the beginning, they urged men to volunteer, sometimes giving white feathers to young men not in uniform. The government's call for women workers in 1915 led to thousands of women responding.
- Many women acted as nurses or ambulance drivers (**Voluntary Aid Detachments**) at the various Fronts.
- From 1917, they joined the women's sections of the armed forces (WAACS, WRNS and WRAF) mostly working in offices or kitchens.

*First World War poster*

## The Home Front: the people

- As well as changes to the workforce, the First World War affected people at home in other ways:
  - **Air raids** by German Zeppelins and bombers, and shelling by German battleships, killed over 1500 civilians.
  - **Food shortages** from 1916, because of German **U-boat** warfare, forced the government to form the Women's Land Army; to take over 2.5 million acres of land, using the powers of DORA, and to ration certain foods from early 1918.
- There were more long-term social and political changes in Britain because of the war:
  - The sacrifices of all classes at home and at the Front led the government to think more about the needs of ordinary people for good housing and education ('a country fit for heroes').
  - In 1918, all men were given the vote.
  - Upper-class families began to lose some of their power, they lost sons at the Front, and great inequalities of wealth became less acceptable. During voluntary rationing, there were strikes in some areas when it seemed the rich were being favoured. After the war, fewer people were prepared to work as servants.
  - Attitudes to women changed as the war showed that women could do virtually any job as well as men, though most lost their war-time jobs to returning soldiers. Partly in recognition of their war-work, most women over thirty were given the vote in 1918. This was extended to all women in 1928.

*A woman munitions worker during the First World War*

## The end of the War

- During 1915 and 1916, the stalemate on the Western Front continued despite new weapons like gas, tanks, aircraft.
- In March 1917, revolution in Russia began to ease pressure on German troops on the Eastern Front. In April, the **USA** joined the Allies. Troops did not arrive at once, but Allied morale was boosted.
- A second revolution in Russia in November 1917 saw massive desertions from the army. In March 1918, Russia pulled out of the war after the **Treaty of Brest–Litovsk**.
- This allowed for the switch of German troops from the Eastern to the Western Front for a surprise offensive on 21 March 1918. The German commanders, Field-Marshall Hindenburg and General Ludendorff, saw this **Spring**, or **Ludendorff**, **Offensive**, as Germany's last chance to win because:
  - large numbers of US troops had been arriving on the Western Front since late 1917;
  - the German army's morale was low;
  - the Allied naval blockade was causing terrible food shortages in Germany.
- The Germans were initially successful when they used the more mobile 'storm troops' to break through Allied lines. The offensive failed because:
  - there was no overall plan
  - the Allies successfully retreated and regrouped
  - German supplies were limited and there were no reserves
  - the Allies were well-supplied
  - the Allies were reinforced with US troops
  - the Allies' effective use of tanks enabled them to launch a successful counter-offensive in August.
- The German troops were pushed back beyond their March 1918 lines. The German commanders realised an **armistice** (ceasefire) was necessary. It was signed on 11 November 1918.

## The First World War (5–8)

1. What do the initials 'DORA' stand for? (1)
2. Name the Minister of War behind the volunteer recruiting campaigns of 1914 and 1915. (1)
3. Which Liberal politician was made Minister for Munitions, in order to solve the 'shell shortage' of 1915? (1)
4. In what year did the British government begin conscription? (1)
5. Who were known as 'conchies'? (1)
6. When did the government form the Women's Land Army? (1)
7. Look at the table below. Which two areas of employment saw the greatest increase of women from 1914 to 1918? (2)

**Women's employment in Britain, 1914 and 1918**

| | 1914 | 1918 |
|---|---|---|
| Munitions | 212,000 | 947,000 |
| Transport | 18,000 | 117,000 |
| Business | 505,000 | 935,000 |
| Agriculture | 190,000 | 228,000 |
| Government and teaching | 262,000 | 460,000 |
| Hotels and catering | 181,000 | 220,000 |
| Industry | 2,179,000 | 2,971,000 |
| Servants | 1,658,000 | 1,250,000 |
| Self-employed | 430,000 | 470,000 |
| Nursing and secretarial | 542,000 | 652,000 |

8. Explain briefly what is meant by 'total war'. (2)
9. What steps did the government take on the Home Front to overcome the food shortages caused by U-boat warfare? (3)
10. Describe briefly how the First World War affected British finances and industries. (3)
11. Give *four* reasons which help explain why Germany finally lost the war. (4)

# ANSWERS & TUTORIALS

SCORE

**1** Defence of the Realm Act. (1)
Passed August 1914.

**2** Lord Kitchener. (1)

**3** Lloyd George. (1)

**4** 1916. (1) The Military Service Act.

**5** Conscientious objectors *or* 'COs' *or* people refusing to be conscripted. (1)

**6** February 1917. (1)

**7** Industry and munitions. (2)

**8** A war which involves or affects everyone in a country (1) with air-raid casualties, rationing. (1)
Other examples: governments take emergency powers (DORA); censorship; takeover of land; conscription.

**9** Formed the Women's Land Army (1). Took over 2.5 million acres of land as allotments for growing food (1). Introduced rationing. (1)
This question asks about the Home Front, so don't write about convoy systems.

**10** Britain's finances were ruined. (1) Older industries (coal, iron, shipbuilding) found world competition difficult after war contracts ended. (1) Newer industries (electronics, aircraft) were boosted by the war. (1)

**11** Fighting a two-front war had weakened Germany – heavy casualties and falling supplies. (1) By 1918, the morale of German troops and civilians was very low. (1) US entry (1917) meant greater supplies and new troops for the Allies by mid-1918. (1) By 1918, Allied commanders were at last using tanks effectively to end the stalemate on the Western Front. (1) The Allied naval blockade limited supplies for German industry and food for civilians. (1)

TOTAL

## What problems faced the peacemakers in 1919?

- In 1919, the leaders of Britain, France and the USA met in Paris to decide the future of Germany and the rest of Europe after the war. There were many problems.
- **Germany** had almost defeated the Allies virtually on its own, so the Allies wanted to make sure it would never be strong enough to fight another war. Also, there was **political chaos in Germany**:
  - the Kaiser had fled and the new government was weak
  - communist and socialist uprisings, inspired by the Bolshevik example in Russia, were breaking out in Berlin and Munich.
- **Nationalism** in central and eastern Europe, and especially in the Austro–Hungarian Empire, was leading to uprisings and attempts to create new independent countries in Yugoslavia, Poland and Czechoslovakia. In Hungary, there was a communist-led revolution.
- **Near-starvation** and **economic ruin** affected large parts of Europe, especially Germany. The Allies continued their naval blockade until the treaties were signed. Such suffering was made worse by the 'flu epidemic of 1919.
- Many people in Allied countries wanted **revenge against Germany** for the:
  - millions killed or injured
  - industrial disruption
  - destruction of villages, towns and farmland, especially in France and Belgium.
- **Secret promises** of land had been made to Italy and Japan to persuade them to join the Allies. These countries now expected their reward.
- There were **differences** between the Allies about what should be done. The war had ended suddenly before any real discussions about peace.

# THE PEACE TREATIES (2)

- Britain, France and the USA (**the Big Three**) made most of the important decisions about the peace treaties. The defeated countries (Germany, Austria–Hungary, Turkey, Bulgaria) were excluded from the talks. But the Big Three had differing ideas :

- **Britain** was led by **David Lloyd George**. He was successful in the 1918 general election, when many had called for Germany to be punished. Lloyd George wanted to enlarge the British Empire by taking Germany's overseas colonies, but he wanted a **compromise peace**, so that Germany:
  - would not want revenge in the future
  - could rebuild its economy and resume trade with Britain
  - would be strong enough to resist communism.

*Lloyd George*

- **France** was led by **Georges Clemenceau**. France had suffered greatly, so he wanted a **harsh peace**. He wanted Germany to be made too weak ever to invade France again, by forcing it to:
  - pay a huge fine for all of France's war damage and debts
  - give up large sections of land and industry
  - disarm almost completely

*Clemenceau*

- **The USA** was led by **Woodrow Wilson**. He wanted a **just peace**, based on his **Fourteen Points**, issued in January 1918. Wilson wanted self-determination (independence) for the different nationalities and a League of Nations to prevent future wars.

- Lloyd George and Clemenceau thought Wilson too idealistic. Wilson was ill during the Conference, and was losing control of the US Congress.

*Wilson*

## The terms of the treaties

- After the peace negotiations ended, **five separate treaties** were signed between the Allies and the defeated countries.
- The **Treaty of Versailles** (June 1919) was the first and most important as it dealt with Germany. Its main points were:
  - **Territory** Germany lost several areas of land in Europe:
    **Alsace–Lorraine** returned to France and the **Saar** to France for 15 years
    **Upper Silesia** and **West Prussia** to Poland as a 'corridor' to the sea, and **Danzig**, which became a Free City under League of Nations control. These losses split East Prussia from the rest of Germany.
    **North Schleswig** to Denmark and **Eupen-Malmédy** to Belgium.
    **The Rhineland**, land between France and a line 50 km east of the Rhine, to be demilitarised.
    **Anschluss** (union) with Austria was forbidden.
  - **Colonies** All Germany's colonies in Africa and the Pacific were handed over to Britain, France or Japan under League of Nations mandates.
  - **Armed Forces** To keep Germany weak, it was only allowed an army of 100,000 (all volunteers, conscription was forbidden), a small navy (six battleships and no submarines); tanks and military aircraft were forbidden.
  - **War Guilt** and **Reparations** Germany was forced to accept Article 231, blaming it for starting the war. The final figure for **reparations** (compensation) was fixed in 1921 at £6,600 million.
- In addition to these and other specific points, a **League of Nations** was set up, but Germany was not allowed to join.
- Most Germans saw this as a **Diktat** (dictated peace).
- The four other treaties dealt with Germany's defeated allies. The Austro–Hungarian Empire was split into several countries, Austria and Hungary becoming two separate states.

- **Treaty of St Germain, 1919** was signed with **Austria**:
  - Austria lost territory to Italy (South Tyrol, Istria), Poland, Czechoslovakia and Yugoslavia (the Successor States)
  - the Austrian army was reduced
  - Anschluss (union) with Germany was forbidden.
- **Treaty of Trianon, 1920** was signed with **Hungary**:
  - territory went to Czechoslovakia, Yugoslavia and Romania.
  - the Hungarian army was reduced.
- **Treaty of Neuilly, 1919** was signed with **Bulgaria**:
  - territory was lost to Greece, Romania and Yugoslavia
  - the Bulgarian army was reduced
- **Treaty of Sèvres, 1920** was signed with **Turkey**:
  - its empire (in the Middle East) was lost to Britain and France under League of Nations mandates.
  - nearly all its European land was lost to Greece
  - reparations were to be paid to the Allies.

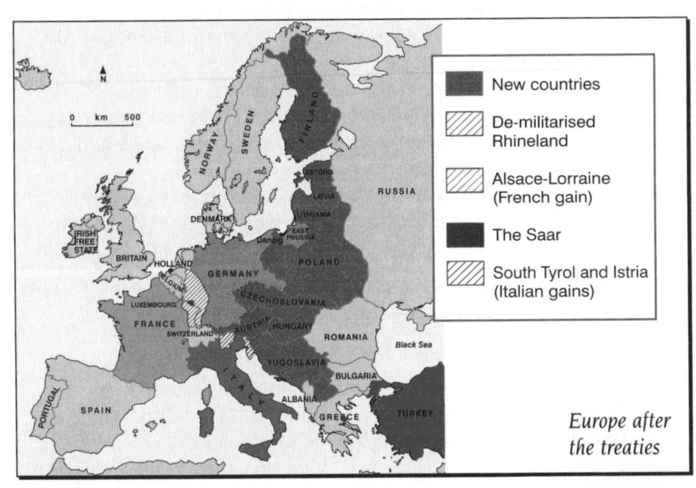


*Europe after the treaties*

## How did the people of Europe react to the treaties?

- Perhaps understandably, reactions in **Germany** were strongest. People objected to:
  - losing so much land, population and industry in Europe
  - losing all their colonies
  - the reductions and restrictions on their armed forces
  - having to accept total blame for the war
  - the way the Treaty of Versailles was forced on them
  - the lack of self-determination for Germans and German-speakers in the new 'successor states'
  - exclusion from the League of Nations
  - the amount of reparations.
- Historians are divided as to just how unfair the treaty was:
  - some see it as **unfair**, because it was not based on the Fourteen Points, and because it punished the German people who had had little power to influence the Kaiser and his government
  - others see it as reasonably **fair**, arguing Germany did not lose that much territory and pointing to how quickly the German economy revived in the 1920s.
- Problems soon arose:
  - In 1922, the German government said it was unable to pay the next instalment of reparation payments as there was near-starvation in parts of Germany.
  - In 1923, France and Belgium sent troops to occupy **the Ruhr**, Germany's main industrial area. Germany resorted to 'passive resistance' with strikes and non-cooperation. The French deported 150,000 striking Germans and killed 132 people in separate incidents.
- These problems caused the collapse of the German currency and **hyper-inflation**. This affected the French economy, leading to France's withdrawal and the **Dawes Plan, 1924** which spread reparation payments according to Germany's ability to pay.

# THE PEACE TREATIES (6)

- Other **defeated powers** were unhappy with the peace treaties:
  - **Hungary** The Treaty of Trianon was not signed until the Communist uprising was replaced by a right-wing dictatorship. There was resentment at the loss of about two-thirds of Hungary's territory.
  - **Turkey** The harsh Treaty of Sèvres led to a successful nationalist revolution led by Mustafa Kemal (Ataturk), which forced the Allies to sign the **Treaty of Lausanne** in 1923. This returned much of the land given to Greece in 1920.

*Mustafa Kemal inspects his troops during the war with Greece, 1922*

- Some of the **Allies** were unhappy with the treaties:
  - **Italy** was angry that much of the Austrian land promised in 1915 in the secret Treaty of London was given to Yugoslavia.
  - **France**, which still feared Germany, wanted a harsher treaty, and needed reparation repayments to pay off war-debts.
  - **Britain** soon thought the treaties, especially Versailles, were too harsh. British governments moved away from France's more hard-line policy such as the occupation of the Ruhr.
- The **USA** moved towards **isolationism**. The US Congress refused to agree to the treaties or to join the League of Nations.

## The Peace Treaties (1–6)

1. Why, by 1919, were many parts of Europe facing near-starvation? (1)
2. Why was the desire for revenge strongest in France and Belgium? (1)
3. Which country, along with Britain and France, made up the 'Big Three' at the negotiations in Paris in 1919? (1)
4. Who was Britain's prime minister during these negotiations? (1)
5. Name the US president who issued the Fourteen Points in January 1918. (1)
6. Why did the British government particularly object to Point 2 of the Fourteen Points, which called for freedom of the seas in peace and war? (1)
7. What was the name of the treaty which Germany had to sign in June 1919? (1)
8. By what other name is the controversial Article 231 of this treaty usually known? (1)
9. What was the significance of Article 231? (2)
10. Why was the French government unhappy about the decisions made concerning the Rhineland? (2)
11. Why were many Germans particularly unhappy about the territorial losses to Poland? (2)
12. Name the *three* countries in the Middle East which Britain took over after the Turkish Empire was broken up. (3)
13. What potential problems existed concerning the new central and east European countries created by the treaties of 1919–20? (3)

# ANSWERS & TUTORIALS

SCORE

1 The Allied naval blockade of Germany. (1)

2 Deaths and injuries, destruction of towns, farmland and roads, had been much greater in these countries. (1) French deaths were almost 1.5 million.

3 The USA. (1)

4 David Lloyd George. (1)

5 Woodrow Wilson. (1)

6 The British naval blockade of Germany played a big part in the Allied victory. (1) By 1919, Germany faced near-starvation.

7 Treaty of Versailles. (1)

8 War-guilt clause. (1)

9 By making Germany accept total blame for the war (1), the Allies were able to justify their demands for reparations. (1) £6600 million was agreed in 1921, but Germany paid much less than this in the end.

10 They had wanted the Rhineland separated from Germany (1), to act as a buffer zone between France and Germany. (1) The compromise was that the Rhineland be demilitarised permanently, with Allied troops in occupation for 15 years.

11 They lost valuable territory (including the coalfields of Upper Silesia and the city of Danzig). (1) The 'Polish Corridor' split East Prussia from the rest of Germany. (1) Over a million Germans were made citizens of Poland. (1)

12 Palestine. (1) Iraq. (1) Jordan. (1)

13 Many were small and weak. (1) Many (especially Poland and Czechoslovakia) had large proportions of different national groups. (1). The loss of territory, industry and population to these countries created much nationalist resentment in Germany. (1) These problems were later exploited by Hitler.

TOTAL

## Germany after the War, 1918–1923

- In late 1918, Germany's desperate condition, its army defeated, its people near starvation and the country in financial ruin, led to mutinies and uprisings all over Germany. The Kaiser fled and abdicated.
- **Ebert**, leader of the Social Democrats (SPD) set up a provisional government. He declared Germany a republic, signed the armistice and called an election in January 1919.
- In Berlin, revolutionary socialists, called **Spartacists**, tried to start a revolution similar to the Bolshevik revolution of November 1917 in Russia. But Ebert used the **Freikorps** to crush them. The Spartacist survivors formed the German Communist Party (KPD) and remained bitter enemies of the SPD.
- The unrest in Berlin forced the new government to meet in Weimar, hence the name **Weimar Republic**, where it drew up a new democratic constitution. This gave the vote to all people over twenty; used proportional representation (PR) for elections to the **Reichstag** (parliament); freedom of speech, of travel, of religious belief were guaranteed and gave the President power to rule without the Reichstag in an emergency (**rule by decree**). PR meant that many small parties were elected, so all Weimar governments were coalitions and usually short-lived.
- The frequent changes of government coincided with many serious problems between 1919 and 1923:
  - Anger at the Treaty of Versailles led to hatred of the Weimar Republic ('**November Criminals**' who had '**stabbed the army in the back**').
  - Many Germans, especially civil servants, judges, police and army officers, were opposed to democracy. This resulted in much right-wing violence, including the **Kapp Putsch** in 1920 and political murders.
  - The **French occupation of the Ruhr, 1923** led to **hyper-inflation** and the collapse of the German currency. Middle-class Germans blamed the Weimar government and so gave it little support.

## The Weimar Republic, 1923–1930

- By 1923, the problems of Weimar Germany were:
  - economic (hyper-inflation)
  - bad relations with Britain and France
  - violent opposition from the extreme left and right.
- From 1923 until 1929, **Stresemann** dominated German politics. He began Germany's **economic recovery** by:
  - calling off passive resistance to the French occupation of the Ruhr
  - introducing a new currency (the **rentenmark**)
  - curbing inflation, so allowing industry to revive and unemployment to fall.
  - negotiating the **Dawes Plan, 1924**, which spread reparation payments according to Germany's ability to pay and secured US loans for German industries.
  - negotiating the **Young Plan, 1929**, which spread reparations even further.
- Stresemann improved Germany's diplomatic position by :
  - persuading France to agree to the Dawes Plan
  - signing the **Locarno Pact, 1925**, by which Germany agreed to respect the western borders agreed at the Treaty of Versailles and to keep the Rhineland demilitarised. The Allies then gradually withdrew their occupation troops.
  - persuading the Allies to allow Germany to join the **League of Nations, 1926**.
- These foreign policy successes helped economic improvement. Foreigners began to invest in Germany. New industries sprang up. By 1929, Germany was the most advanced industrial nation after the USA.
- These successes were what right-wing opponents of Weimar had wanted, so support for extreme parties dropped considerably.
- But in 1929 Stresemann died. This and the **Wall Street Crash** in the US, which meant that loans from the US had to be repaid, resulted in a drastic rise in unemployment to six million by 1932.

## Hitler and the Nazis, 1918–1930

- Hitler was an Austrian, born in 1889. He fought in the German army in the First World War. In 1919, after the defeat of a Communist uprising in Munich, he was sent there by the army to spy on the small German Workers Party (DAP). Hitler decided to join this party and to take it over.
- In 1920, the party became the NSDAP or **Nazis**, adopting a **25-point Programme**, partly written by Hitler. This had elements of nationalism, socialism and anti-Semitism. In 1921, Hitler became leader of the Nazi Party. The party adopted a new party flag he designed with a swastika symbol.
- Hitler was a powerful speaker. He played on anger against the Treaty of Versailles and economic hardship. He blamed these problems on the Weimar government, Communists and Jews.
- He also formed the **Stormtroopers** (SA) or **Brownshirts**, named for their uniforms. Many were ex-soldiers and unemployed. They used violence to break up the political meetings and demonstrations of their opponents.
- Public speeches in beer halls, propaganda and SA violence led to the growth of Nazism in southern Germany. By 1923 the party had had over 50,000 members.

*SA – Sturm Abteilung (stormtroopers)*

- When Stresemann ended passive resistance to the French occupation of the Ruhr in 1923, German nationalists were furious, especially the Nazis.
- Hitler decided to begin a national revolution against the Weimar government in Berlin. The plan was to take over Munich and Bavaria, where Nazi strength was greatest, and from there begin a **March on Berlin**.
- In November 1923, Hitler and the SA took over a Munich beer hall (the **Beer-Hall**, or Munich, **Putsch**) where the Bavarian leader, and the army and police chiefs were addressing a meeting. Hitler was supported by General Ludendorff, a First World War hero. These Bavarian officials were persuaded to support Hitler's plan, but they soon changed their minds. A Nazi/SA march in Munich was blocked by police and shooting broke out. One policeman and sixteen Nazis were killed.
- Hitler was put on trial for treason, but the judge allowed him to make long, political speeches which were widely reported. He received a light sentence. Hitler wrote ***Mein Kampf*** in Landsberg Prison. In it he set out his beliefs and plans. They were racist, nationalist, anti-communist and anti-democratic.
- Hitler was released in December 1924, and found Stresemann's policies had greatly improved the German economy. 1924–30 became known as the Nazis' 'Lean Years' because of their poor election results.
- Hitler used this period to reorganise the Nazi Party. Power was centralised under him and sections were set up to recruit more members, for example, students, teachers, Hitler Youth.
- Hitler also decided the Nazis would have to use elections to win power, not just violence as in 1923. In 1925 Hitler set up the black-uniformed **SS** (Schutz Staffel), a sign that street violence would continue.

## Germany, 1918–1945 (1–4)

**1** Name the Social Democrat politician who took over the government of Germany after the Kaiser fled and abdicated. (1)

**2** What were the Freikorps? (1)

**3** Why did many Germans refer to the Weimar politicians as the 'November Criminals'? (1)

**4** How was the right-wing Kapp Putsch of 1920 defeated? (1)

**5** How did Stresemann deal with the hyper-inflation resulting from the French occupation of the Ruhr in 1923? (1)

**6** Why did France agree to the Dawes Plan, 1924, which spread the amount of reparations paid by Germany? (1)

**7** What did Germany promise when signing the Locarno Pact in 1925? (1)

**8** Name *one* of the new industries developed in Germany in the 1920s with the aid of foreign loans and investments. (1)

**9** What is anti-Jewish racism often known as? (1)

**10** In what year did Hitler become leader of the Nazi Party? (1)

**11** What were the SA? (2)

**12** What happened when, in November 1923, the Nazis tried to overthrow the Weimar government? (2)

**13** What problems were the Nazi Party experiencing when Hitler was released from prison at the end of 1924? (3)

**14** Why were the Nazis generally unsuccessful between 1924 and 1930? (3)

*Feeding hungry people in Germany after the First World War*

# ANSWERS & TUTORIALS

SCORE

**1** Ebert. (1)

**2** Right-wing ex-soldiers. (1)

**3** They hated them for the armistice of November 1918. (1)

**4** By the workers of Berlin holding a general strike. (1)

**5** He ended passive resistance. (1) *or* He introduced a new currency, the rentenmark. (1)

**6** The occupation of the Ruhr had not achieved what they wanted, so regular, smaller reparation payments spread over a longer period were better than none. (1)

**7** To respect their western frontiers. (1) *or* To keep German troops out of the Rhineland. (1)

**8** Any *one* from: cars *or* radios *or* telephones *or* airships *or* ocean liners. (1)

**9** Anti-Semitism. (1) Such ideas were widespread in many parts of Europe, not just Germany.

**10** 1921. (1)

**11** The Nazis' Stormtroopers or Brownshirts. (1) They used violence to break up opponents' meetings . (1)

**12** Their march on Berlin was stopped by the police. (1) Hitler was later arrested, tried and put in prison. (1)

**13** They were banned after the Beer-Hall Putsch. (1) They had split into factions. (1) Strasser challenged Hitler, he wanted to emphasise the socialist aspects of Nazism. (1) Hitler changed the Nazi Programme, so confiscation of private property without compensation applied only to Jews.

**14** Stresemann's economic policies stopped inflation and revived industry. (1) The Dawes Plan 1924 and Young Plan 1929 arranged for loans from the US to Germany. (1) Stresemann's foreign policy resulted in the removal of Allied troops from the Rhineland and the admission of Germany to the League of Nations, 1926. (1)

TOTAL

## How did Hitler win power in Germany in 1933?

- The Wall Street Crash in 1929 and the **Depression** caused great problems in Germany:
  - **economic** and **social**, with high unemployment and poverty
  - **political**, as coalition governments, unable to agree on policies, changed more frequently. President Hindenburg increasingly used his power to rule by decree.
- Many conservative Germans, who already disliked the Weimar government, turned to more extreme right-wing parties. The Nazis won 107 seats in 1930. At the same time, many working-class people turned to the Communists, who also hated the Weimar Republic. They won 77 seats in 1930.
- **Nazi violence** by the SA was important. It made the Weimar government look as if it could not keep law and order, and created the impression that the Nazis were organised and willing to take strong action against Communists. As wealthy business people were scared of Communism and jealous of the Jews, donations to the Nazis increased.
- **Nazis promises** to make Germany great again, as it had been under the Kaiser, won more supporters.
- **Propaganda**, organised by Goebbels, and Hitler's speaking powers brought increasing support for the Nazis. In April 1932, Hitler stood against Hindenburg in the Presidential elections, and won 13 million votes to Hindenburg's 19 million. In the elections of July 1932, the Nazis became the largest single party with 230 seats.
- In the elections of November 1932, the Nazis dropped to 196 seats, while the Communists rose yet again to 100.
- Early in 1933, von Papen persuaded Hindenburg to appoint Hitler as Chancellor of a conservative-dominated coalition government. On 30 January, Hitler became Chancellor (prime minister) of Germany.

## Hitler's dictatorship

- Hitler quickly called new elections for March 1933. The SA used violence against anti-Nazis, especially Communists.
- Just before the election, the Reichstag caught fire (the **Reichstag Fire**). Hitler blamed the Communists, and ordered their arrest. The Nazis only had an overall majority by banning elected Communists.
- Hitler quickly made Germany a **totalitarian dictatorship**.
  - **March** The **Enabling Act** gave Hitler the power to rule by decree for four years
  - **April** Nazi officials (**gauleiters**) took charge of the eighteen provinces of Germany.
  - **May** All trade unions were banned
  - **July** After months of attacks, all opposition parties were banned and many more political opponents put in concentration camps
- By early 1934 Germany was under Nazi control, but Hitler faced opposition from **Roehm**, leader of the SA. Like Strasser in the 1920s, Roehm's supporters wanted Hitler to carry out the more left-wing policies of the Nazi Programme. Roehm's plan for the SA to takeover the army worried the generals.
- In June 1934, to reassure the army, Hitler ordered the **Night of the Long Knives**, in which the SS murdered Roehm and other SA leaders.
- After Hindenburg died in August, the army supported Hitler becoming **Führer** (combining the jobs of President, Commander-in-Chief of the army and Chancellor).
- Opposition became difficult. The **Gestapo** (secret police) and the SS used informers, Block Leaders, and arrests to intimidate potential opponents.
- Goebbels used **censorship**, as well as **propaganda**. No criticism could be published; cheap radios ensured Nazi views were heard by all; loudspeakers appeared in streets; and the mass **Nuremberg Rallies** were filmed for cinemas.

## Germany 1918–1945 (5–6)

**1** Give *one* reason why so many Germans hated the Weimar Republic by 1932. (1)

**2** How large, approximately, was the SA by 1932? (1)

**3** Name *one* thing which made the Nazis seem a well-ordered and disciplined force. (1)

**4** Why did so many middle-class and wealthy business people make donations to the Nazi Party? (1)

**5** How many Germans were unemployed by 1932? (1)

**6** What was Goebbels in charge of during the early 1930s? (1)

**7** Which conservative German politician persuaded Hindenburg to appoint Hitler as Chancellor? (1)

**8** When did Hitler finally become Chancellor of Germany? (1)

**9** How was Goering, who was in charge of the police, able to help the Nazis in the run-up to the March 1933 elections? (2)

**10** What was the importance of the Reichstag Fire on 27 February 1933? (2)

**11** Why was the Enabling Act (March 1933) so important in the destruction of the democracy of the Weimar Republic? (2)

**12** Why did Hitler decide to have the SA leaders murdered during the Night of the Long Knives? (3)

**13** Apart from censorship and propaganda, how else did the Nazis try to prevent opposition? (3)

*Nazi rally at Nuremberg*

# ANSWERS & TUTORIALS

SCORE

1 Any *one* from: Signing the Treaty of Versailles *or* hyper-inflation *or* weak coalition governments unable to solve economic problems. (1)

2 450,000 (1) In 1929 there were fewer than 30,000 in the SA.

3 Any *one* from: uniforms and flags *or* well-drilled processions and rallies *or* well-planned attacks on opponents. (1)

4 They were frightened of communism and the Nazis were violently anti-Communist. (1)

5 6 million. (1)

6 Propaganda. (1) Especially by torchlight processions, large rallies, radio and film.

7 Von Papen. (1) The political and economic elites thought they could control Hitler.

8 January 1933. (1)

9 He enrolled the SA as special constables. (1) He organised a wave of political violence against the Nazis' opponents. (1)

10 Hitler ordered the arrest of thousands of Communists. (1) Hindenburg agreed to Hitler's Reichstag Fire Decree which suspended civil and political rights. (1)

11 Hitler could make laws by-passing the Reichstag and the President. (1) He rushed through measures against trade unions and political parties which, in five months, turned Germany into a dictatorship. (1)

12 He wanted supreme power but Roehm and the SA were potential rivals. (1) Hitler did not like the left-wing policies favoured by Roehm. (1) He was afraid that Roehm's plans to take over the army would lead to army opposition. (1)

13 They tried to set up a 'Reich Church' of Nazi supporters, shutdown Catholic Youth groups and arrested religious opponents. (1) The Gestapo and SS created an atmosphere of fear and suspicion. (1) Opponents were shut up in concentration camps. (1) The Nazis encouraged children to spy and inform on their parents.

TOTAL

## Women and children

- The Nazis had clear ideas about how women and children should contribute to the Third Reich.
- **Policies for women** were based on the traditional German '**3Ks**': Kinder, Kirche, Kücher (children, church, kitchen):
  - making women stay at home and have children. They were encouraged to produce large families with **loans** and **medals** linked to the number of children.
  - passing laws to remove women from state jobs which were then given to unemployed men. Nazis did not support equality for women, no woman had a top job in the Nazi Party.
  - trying to control women's fashions and appearance so they conformed to the Nazis' traditional view of women. Make-up, hair-dyeing, high heels and smoking were discouraged.
- **Policies for children** were designed to ensure that the next generation, especially boys, would support Hitler and the Nazis.
  - Schools were put under national control with a national curriculum. All teachers had to swear loyalty to Hitler, and join the Nazi Teachers' League. Those who refused were sacked, as were Jewish teachers.
  - The **curriculum** was altered, giving particular emphasis to **History**, all pre-Nazi textbooks were banned and children were taught how the Nazis were saving Germany;
    **Biology**, where Nazi racism was taught as a false 'race science' which said that Aryans were superior and other races inferior; and **PE**, time spent on PE was tripled to ensure fitter soldiers and mothers.
  - Young people's lives outside school were also controlled. They were expected to join one of the Nazi Youth movements for boys and girls of all ages.

## The Nazi economy

- Hitler and the Nazis had three aims for the German economy:
  - reducing unemployment
  - re-arming Germany
  - making Germany self-sufficient.
- **Unemployment** was dealt with in several ways:
  - a **National Labour Service**, set up before 1933, was expanded, using government money to fund public works programmes like building motorways, houses, schools. From 1935, this became compulsory for six months for all 18 to 25 year olds.
  - the jobs of Jews and women forced out of employment were given to unemployed men. The thousands in concentration camps were not counted as unemployed.
- **Re-armament** began, first secretly then, after 1935, openly. Thousands of aircraft, tanks, battleships were built, and the army increased by conscription from 100,000 to 1,400,000. These policies also helped reduce unemployment.
- **Self-sufficiency** was encouraged by:
  - increasing agricultural production,
  - controlling imports
  - finding substitutes for foreign imports, which also provided work.
- Schacht was Minister of the Economy until 1937. He was replaced by Goering whose **Four-Year Plan** was to prepare Germany for war.
- Trade unions were abolished in 1933, workers had to join the Nazi **German Labour Front**. Strikes were illegal, wages were low and limits on hours of work were lifted so many people worked over sixty hours a week.

*Men in the Labour Front*

## Did most Germans support Hitler?

- It is difficult to assess how many Germans supported Hitler In his dictatorship. In the last free elections in Germany in November 1933, the Nazis had only 34 per cent of the vote. In March 1933, despite violence and intimidation against their oppostion, the Nazis still only got 43 per cent of the vote.
- Many Germans, who were not Jewish, Socialist or Communist, were happy with Nazi policies on unemployment and German re-armament.
- Despite Gestapo terror and Nazi propaganda, there were people who **resisted** Hitler's regime:
  - **Communists and Social Democrats** set up underground organisations, publishing newsletters, sabotaging production
  - **Young people** who hated the Hitler Youth movements instead joined rebel groups, such as the Swing, the Edelweiss Pirates; or the White Rose Group which published anti-Nazi leaflets.
  - **Religious groups and individuals** opposed persecution of Jews and euthanasia of the mentally-ill.
  - **The Army**, especially in the last years of the war, feared Hitler was leading Germany to destruction. The most famous resistance from the Army was the Bomb Plot in 1944.
  - **Upper-class Germans** had initially supported the Nazis because they were anti-Communist, but were alienated by Nazi corruption
- The Nazis lost support as the war went on. Germany was not prepared for a long war. From 1939 there was rationing because of **food shortages** and from 1942 people suffered increasingly heavy **bombing**.
- As the war continued, hardship increased. By 1945, Germany was in ruins.

## Hitler and racism

- Hitler and the Nazis were deeply **racist**. All non-Aryan groups (Jews, blacks, gypsies and Slavs) were considered inferior.
- The Nazis were obsessed with '**racial purity**'. From 1934 they ordered the sterlisation of disabled people and criminals, and killed mentally-ill people.
- It was the **Jews** who were the main target of Nazi racist measures, even though only 1 per cent of Germans were Jewish. They persecuted them by propaganda, laws and violence.
  - **Propaganda** When he became Chancellor, Hitler spread the Nazis' ideas through 'race science', posters, films and textbooks.
  - **Laws**
    **1933** All Jews were banned from state jobs; the SA and SS organised a **boycott** of all Jewish-owned shops.
    **1935 Nuremberg Laws** removed German citizenship from Jewish people.
    **1936–41** Further laws restricted Jewish education and property-ownership, and enforced segregation.
  - **Violence**
    **Kristallnacht** (Night of Broken Glass) **November 1938** The SA and SS attacked Jewish homes, shops and synagogues after a German diplomat was shot in Paris by a Jewish student. After a week of terror, the Nazis imposed a fine of one billion marks on the Jews.
  - **The Final Solution** From 1938 to 1941, Jews in Germany and eastern Europe were forced into ghettos and violence against them increased. From July 1941, it was decided to eliminate all Jews. Himmler and the SS were to carry this out, first by special SS squads, then in a more organised way in **extermination camps** (for example, Auschwitz). Six million Jews were murdered.
- The Nazis also murdered other groups of people they considered racially inferior: Slavs, gypsies (Sinti and Roma) and homosexuals – another five million people.

## Germany 1918–1945 (7–10)

**1** What were the '3Ks' of Nazi propaganda about the role of women? (1)

**2** Why were many women teachers and all women doctors sacked after 1933? (1)

**3** How were loans, given to couples on marriage, used to encourage large families? (1)

**4** Why, after 1937, did the Nazis begin to change their policies about women and work? (1)

**5** Name *one* of the school subjects that the Nazis emphasised in their new national curriculum. (1)

**6** What do the following groups have in common: Pimpfen, League of German Girls and Hitler Youth? (1)

**7** Did the Communist and Social Democratic parties co-operate in resisting the Nazi dictatorship? (1)

**8** Who were Martin Niemöller and Dietrich Bonhöffer? (1)

**9** What were the Swing groups and the Edelweiss Pirates? 1)

**10** What was the White Rose Group and who were its leaders? (2)

**11** Name *two* groups of people, in addition to Jewish people, which Nazi racism saw as being inferior. (2)

**12** What did the *two* Nuremberg Laws of 1935 do? (2)

**13** What happened to Jewish people in Kristallnacht in November 1938? (2)

**14** What was the 'Final Solution' decided by leading Nazis in July 1941 at the Wannsee Conference? (3)

*A prisoner at Belsen concentration camp*

SCORE

**1** Children, Church, Cooking. (1)

**2** Unemployed men could have their jobs. (1) *or* Women could concentrate on having children. (1)

**3** The more children a couple had, the less they had to repay. (1) The woman had to give up her job.

**4** The war preparations of re-armament and conscription led to a labour shortage. (1)

**5** Any *one* from: History *or* Biology *or* PE. (1)

**6** They were all Nazi Youth movements. (1) From 1936 membership was virtually compulsory.

**7** No. (1) This had much to do with the bitterness surrounding the suppression of the Spartacist Revolt of 1919. In 1932, these two parties together had outnumbered the Nazis in the Reichstag.

**8** People from religious groups who resisted Nazis. (1)

**9** Youth groups who rejected Nazi culture and involvement with the Hitler youth movements. (1)

**10** An anti-Nazi group of students. (1) Hans and Sophie Scholl / Christoph Probst. (1)

**11** Any *two* from: Slavs *or* black people *or* gypsies. (2)

**12** Took away German citizenship from Jews. (1) Forbade marriage between Jews and Aryans. (1)

**13** Their homes, shops, synagogues were attacked *or* Many were killed or put into concentration camps *or* Jews had to pay a fine of one billion marks. (2) Kristallnacht was carried out by the SA and SS. Ninety-one Jewish people were killed and 20,000 put into concentration camps.

**14** The policy to kill all Jews in Europe. (1) It was carried out by Himmler and the SS. (1) At first, it was carried out by special SS squads (Einsatzgrüppen), then in death camps. (1) Many Jews were used as slave-labour in factories and gassed when they were no longer fit to work.

TOTAL

## Russia in 1900

- In 1900, Russia was a vast empire of sixteen different nationalities and poor communications. There were huge **social divisions**: 80 per cent of the population were poor, uneducated **peasants**, farming small plots by old-fashioned methods. Bad harvests often resulted in famine. The **nobles** (1 per cent) owned a quarter of the land.
- Industrialisation only began at the end of the 19th century, funded by foreign investment. Factories were huge and workers faced awful working and living conditions. Trade unions were banned.

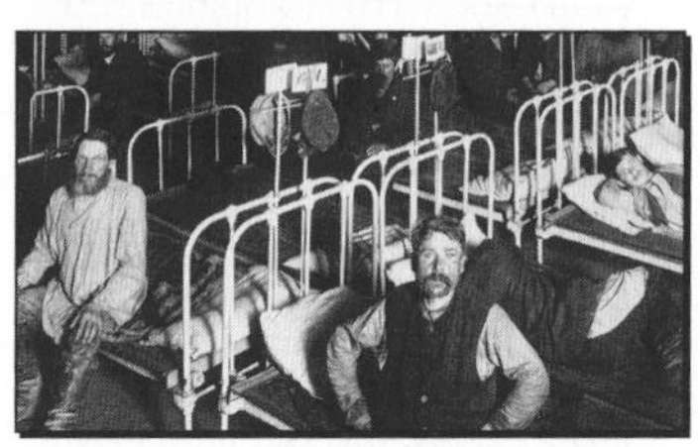

*Industrial workers in Moscow*

- Russia was an **autocracy** ruled by the Tsar (emperor) Nicholas II. There were no elections, parliament, free speech or democracy. The Orthodox Church supported the system which was run by corrupt and inefficient officials and backed by the **Okhrana** (secret police).
- This Tsarist autocracy and the social structure were opposed by people who wanted change. Particularly important were:
  - **Cadets (Constitutional Democrats)** were mainly middle class and wanted a liberal parliamentary democracy.
  - **Social Revolutionaries (SRs)** wanted to give the land to the peasants, who were their main support. They used terror and assassination to try to bring about change.
  - **Social Democrats (RSDLP)** followed Marxist ideas, believing the industrial working class, not peasants, would bring about revolution. In 1903 the party split in two:

    **Mensheviks** wanted a mass party with industrial workers as members and believed a socialist revolution could only happen much later.

    **Bolsheviks**, led by Lenin, wanted a small party with full-time revolutionaries and believed the revolution could be soon.

## Russia, 1905–1914

- Russia's problems were made worse after 1900 by **bad harvests** with hunger in the countryside and an **industrial depression** with unemployment and wage cuts in the cities.
- The Tsar's government decided to declare war on Japan in 1904, thinking a victory would end the Russian people's discontent. But the **Russo–Japanese War, 1904–5** was a disaster. Russia suffered huge defeats on land and sea. The war caused increased hardship and shortages in Russia, leading to protests, mainly by the 'tame' trade unions, allowed by the Tsar in an attempt to control opposition.
- In January 1905, a large but peaceful demonstration was fired on by troops **(Bloody Sunday)**. This sparked off the **1905 Revolution**. Demonstrations and land seizures spread all over Russia and, in June, sailors mutinied. All the Tsar's opponents seemed united.
- In September, a **general strike** was called, with workers in St Petersburg setting up a **Soviet** (workers' council). This worried the middle class, so Nicholas II quickly issued the **October Manifesto**, promising a **Duma** (parliament), free speech and the freedom to form political parties. The Cadets were satisfied and ended their opposition. The Tsar used troops to crush the revolution. Many were arrested or exiled.
- With the revolution over, Nicholas broke his promises. The **Fundamental Law** gave little power to the Duma, and elections were structured to give most seats to the wealthy. Later Dumas were quickly dismissed for criticising the government. By 1912, the Tsar was again ruling without one.
- Under a new chief minister, Stolypin, there was harsh repression; but also **land reform**. This ended when Stolypin was assassinated in 1911.

## The Revolutions of 1917

- Stolypin's repression and reforms between 1905 and 1911 reduced protest, but discontent re-emerged between 1911 and 1914.
- As with the Russo–Japanese War, 1904–5, Nicholas II hoped Russian involvement in the **First World War** would quieten his opponents in a wave of patriotism. At first, this seemed to work.
- But massive defeats, the increased influence of **Rasputin** after 1915 when Nicholas took command of the army, and food and fuel shortages in the cities, caused by the lack of agricultural workers and disrupted transport, led to more protests and mutinies.
- In March 1917, strikes and protest demonstrations by women triggered the first stages of the **March Revolution**. The police and army were unable to control the demonstrations. Many soldiers joined the protesters. On 15 March Nicholas II abdicated.
- From March to November, there was **Dual Power**, with two rival authorities, in the new Russian republic:
  - The **Provisional Government** formed by some Duma members as a temporary government.
  - The **Petrograd Soviet** The revived 1905 Soviet was at first dominated by SRs and Mensheviks. They supported the Provisional Government though many workers and soldiers were more loyal to the Soviet.
- The Provisional Government:
  - granted free speech, the release of political prisoners and promised democratic elections for a proper parliament.
  - insisted that Russia should stay in the war until Germany was defeated
  - decided other problems, like peasant demands for land, would have to wait.

The last two decisions were unpopular as most Russians had had enough of the war and peasants and workers wanted immediate reforms.

# The Russian Revolution (4)

- In April, **Lenin**, leader of the **Bolsheviks**, returned to Russia from exile. He played a key role in encouraging a second revolution. By then, workers were occupying factories, peasants were seizing land and elected soviets were appearing all over Russia. The Provisional Government tried to stop this. Lenin wrote his ideas in the **April Theses**, based on two slogans: **All Power to the Soviets** and **Peace, Land and Bread**.
- Before Lenin's arrival, Bolshevik leaders had supported the Provisional Government. Now they were persuaded by Lenin that there should be a revolution.
- In May, **Trotsky** returned to Russia. He had been a Menshevik after the split and then independent from 1904 to 1917. Now, agreeing with Lenin's ideas, he applied to join the Bolsheviks and soon became a leading spokesman for them.
- Soon, more Bolsheviks were elected to the soviets. This success was set back by the **July Days**, when pro-Bolshevik soldiers tried to overthrow the Provisional Government, now led by **Kerensky**. The Bolsheviks were banned and their leaders arrested, but Lenin managed to escape.
- In September, **Kornilov** attempted a coup, first against the soviets, then against the Provisional Government. Kerensky panicked. He released the Bolsheviks and armed their **Red Guards**. Kornilov's attempted coup collapsed. The Bolsheviks increased in popularity and began to win majorities in elections to soviets and city councils.
- In October, Lenin encouraged the Bolsheviks to overthrow Kerensky. The leaders voted 10 to 2 in favour.
- On 6/7 November, the Bolshevik **November Revolution** succeeded and power was handed to an All-Russian Congress of Soviets.

## The Russian Revolution (1–4)

**1** Which social group formed over 80 per cent of the population in Russia in 1900? (1)

**2** What effect did the 50 per cent population increase from 1860–1900 have on the size of peasant land holdings? (1)

**3** Name *one* problem faced by factory workers in Russia by 1900. (1)

**4** Who became Tsar (emperor) of Russia in 1894? (1)

**5** What was the Okhrana? (1)

**6** Name *one* political party which was opposed to Tsarist autocracy in Russia in 1900. (1)

**7** Which political group did Lenin lead from 1903 onwards? (1)

**8** What war from1904–5 helped start the Revolution of 1905? (1)

**9** What was 'Bloody Sunday'? (1)

**10** What was the 'Duma', which Nicholas II promised the Russian people in his October Manifesto of 1905? (1)

**11** What were the *two* main differences between the 1905 Revolution and the March Revolution of 1917? (2)

**12** What were the *two* slogans of Lenin's April Theses in 1917? (2)

**13** Give *one* consequence of the 'July Days' for the Bolsheviks. (1)

**14** Apart from their refusal to end Russia's involvement in the First World War, give *two* other reasons why the Provisional Government became increasingly unpopular in the period March to November 1917? (3)

**15** Why did Lenin urge the Bolsheviks to overthrow the Provisional Government from October 1917? (3)

# ANSWERS & TUTORIALS

SCORE

1 Peasants. (1)

2 They became much smaller. (1)

3 Any *one* from: Bad working conditions *or* low pay *or* poor housing *or* no trade unions. (1)

4 Nicholas II. (1)

5 The Tsar's secret police. (1)

6 Any *one* from: Cadets *or* Social Revolutionaries *or* Social Democrats (1)

7 The Bolsheviks. (1)

8 The Russo–Japanese War. (1)

9 Soldiers fired on a peaceful demonstration wanting to present a petition to the Tsar in January 1905. (1)

10 A parliament. (1) Division among his opponents allowed Nicholas II to use troops to crush the revolution. He soon broke his promises and ruled as an autocrat again.

11 In March 1917, soldiers refused to fire on the demonstrators. (1) The Tsar was forced to abdicate in March 1917. (1) Neither of these happened in 1905.

12 All Power to the Soviets (1) Peace, Land and Bread. (1)

13 Any *one* from: They were banned *or* Their leaders were imprisoned *or* Lenin went into hiding (1)

14 They did not solve the problems of land ownership or food shortages. (1) They did not hold elections for a new parliament. (1) Consequently, more people supported the Soviets, the only freely and regularly elected bodies, leading to 'Dual Power '.

15 From September, the Bolsheviks won majorities in elections to soviets in towns. (1) He was afraid of a military coup. (1) He hoped a revolution in Russia would lead to revolutions elsewhere. (1) With the Provisional Government unpopular and weak, he saw this as the Bolsheviks' best chance of power.

TOTAL

## The Communists and the Civil War, 1917–21

- The All-Russian Congress of Soviets, which had a Bolshevik majority, elected a government (**Sovnarkom**): Lenin was Chairman (prime minister), Trotsky was Commissar for Foreign Affairs and the less well-known Stalin was Commissar for Nationalities.
- Sovnarkom abolished the property rights of noble landowners, promised an immediate end to the war and self-determination for different nationalities.
- Just before his overthrow, Kerensky had set a date for elections to a new **Constituent Assembly**. The Bolsheviks won only 175 seats out of 707 while the SRs won 370. By then the SRs had split and the Left SRs formed a coalition with the Bolsheviks. The Bolsheviks closed down the Assembly as counter-revolution from the Cadets and pro-Tsarist groups threatened.
- The Communists (Bolsheviks) set up the **Cheka** to crush these counter-revolutionary threats.
- The biggest problem for the Communists was the First World War. Peasant soldiers were leaving the Front to share out the land. Lenin argued they should make peace, even though the Germans would impose harsh terms. At first, most Communists disagreed with him.
- The **Treaty of Brest–Litovsk** was signed in March 1918. Trotsky resigned and the Left SRs pulled out of the coalition in protest.
- Russia was now facing civil war between **Reds** (Communists) and **Whites** (anti-Communists). The Allies sent several armies to help the Whites. As the civil war developed between 1918 and 1920, both sides committed atrocities. The Cheka carried out a 'Red Terror' to counter a 'White Terror'.
- At first, it seemed as if the Communists would lose. The Whites had several well-equipped armies and controlled most of Russia. The Communists just had the Red Guards, and controlled only the centre of Russia.

- The Communists had several strengths:
  - Trotsky was appointed Commissar for War. He quickly organised a vast and efficient **Red Army** using ex-Tsarist officers and conscription.
  - They were united, the Whites' leaders saw each other as rivals.
  - Control of the centre of the country meant the Reds could use the railways to shift troops quickly to the various fronts.
  - Most peasants supported the Reds, as a White victory would mean nobles would take back the land.
  - Many Russians supported the Reds out of **patriotism**, as they resented foreign intervention.
- By 1920, the Whites were largely defeated. Poland invaded Russia between 1920 and 1921, this ended with the Treaty of Riga taking much land from Russia.

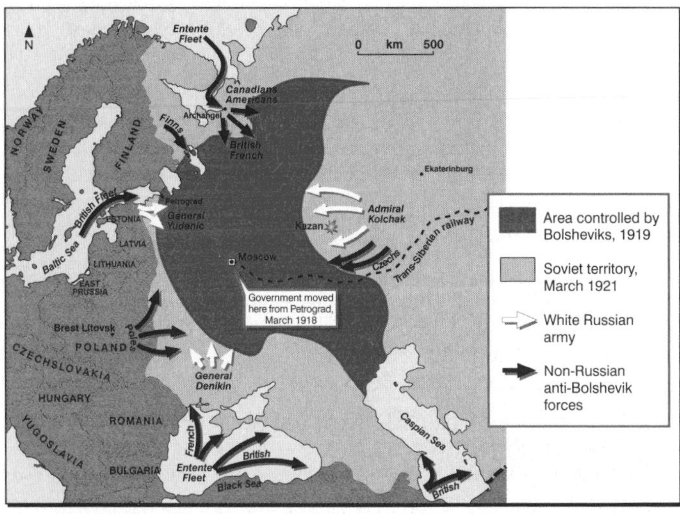


*Russia in the Civil War, 1918–21*

## Lenin's rule, 1917–24

- Before and during the 1917 Revolutions, revolutionary peasants and workers took over land and factories, even though the Communists wanted state farms and nationalised factories run by the government.
- The First World War and the Revolutions disrupted agricultural and industrial production so when the Civil War began the Communists introduced emergency economic measures, known as **War Communism**.
- Under War Communism, the government took over all the factories and forced peasants to hand over surplus food to avoid starvation in the towns. Most peasants hated this. They began to grow less food and to hide any surplus. This, and Civil War disruption, led to famine in many parts of Russia by 1921.
- Some left Communists wanted War Communism to continue after the Civil War, but by 1921 Lenin had come to believe new reforms were needed to revive the economy. His first suggestions were rejected by the Communists.
- Then came the **Kronstadt Rebellion** by sailors and workers in the Kronstadt naval base. This was led mainly by left anarchist groups. They demanded an end to War Communism and a return to full democracy in the soviets. Trotsky was ordered to crush the revolt; thousands of Red Army soldiers and Kronstadt rebels were killed before it was suppressed.

*Red Army soldiers cross the ice to crush the Kronstadt rebels*

- During the crushing of the Kronstadt Rebellion, Lenin persuaded the Communist government to accept his earlier proposals, the **New Economic Policy (NEP)**.
- NEP was controversial as it involved a limited return to capitalism allowing the private sale of some consumer goods and food. Some left Communists opposed NEP strongly, even though the main industries (iron, steel, coal, the railways, banks and foreign trade) remained nationalised.
- Because NEP was seen as dangerous as it revived capitalism, the Communists decided to ban other parties from the soviets and factions within their own party as a temporary emergency measure.
- Under NEP:
  - small factories were returned to former owners or leased out for profit to others.
  - peasants were allowed to sell part of their surplus food for profit.
- By 1924, NEP was proving successful. Agricultural production increased and industry began to return to pre-1913 levels. Some people like **kulaks** (rich peasants) and **nepmen** (businessmen) became very wealthy. This worried many Communists.
- In 1924 a new constitution set up a more centralised federal system, known as the **USSR**. Much of this was drawn up by Stalin. There was strong federal control, though each national group had its own republic.
- In 1922, Stalin was appointed **General Secretary** of the Communist Party. Some of Stalin's actions began to worry Lenin and other Communists, but in 1922 Lenin suffered the first of several strokes. These kept him out of active politics for most of his remaining years. He died in 1924.

## The Russian Revolution (5–8)

**1** What was Sovnarkom? (1)

**2** Who was the first Chairman (prime minister) of the new government? (1)

**3** Which party won the majority of seats in the newly-elected Constituent Assembly? (1)

**4** How did the new government deal with the land question? (1)

**5** What was the Cheka? (1)

**6** Name *one* of the losses imposed on the Russia by Germany in the Treaty of Brest–Litovsk (March 1918)? (1)

**7** What effect did the signing of the Treaty of Brest–Litovsk have on the Russian government? (1)

**8** What was the Czech Legion? (1)

**9** What were the two sides in the Russian Civil War 1918–20 called? (2)

**10** Name *two* of the foreign countries which sent armies to help the anti-communist forces? (2)

**11** How did control of the central railway system help the Communists win the Civil War? (2)

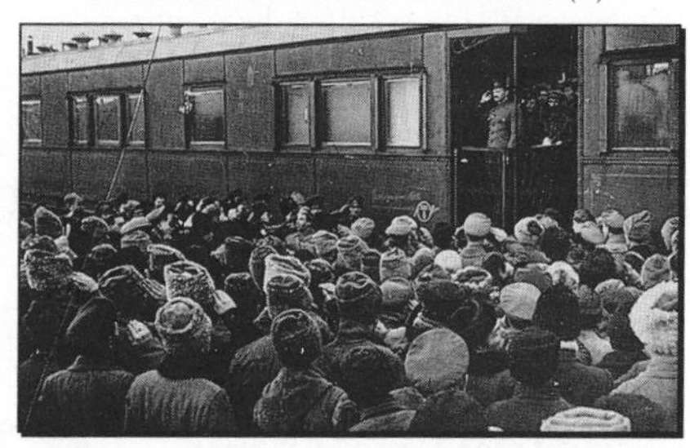

*Trotsky speaking to his troops, 1919*

**12** What were the main features of War Communism? (3)

**13** Give *three* results of the NEP. (3)

# ANSWERS & TUTORIALS

SCORE

**1** The government set up after the Bolshevik Revolution in November 1917. (1)

**2** Lenin. (1)

**3** Social Revolutionaries (1)
The SRs then split into factions (Right and Left), the Left SRs formed a coalition with the Bolsheviks.

**4** It passed a decree (law) which gave the lands of the Tsar, nobility and church to the peasants. (1)

**5** A secret police force set up by the Bolsheviks to deal with counter-revolution. (1)

**6** Any *one* from: 25 per cent of its population *or* 27 per cent of its best farmland *or* 26 per cent of its railways *or* 70 per cent of its iron and coal industries. (1)

**7** The Left SRs left the coalition government *or* the Left SRs began to fight the Bolshevik government *or* Trotsky resigned as Commissar for Foreign Affairs. (1) The Bolsheviks were deeply divided – some even considered arresting Lenin.

**8** A force of Czech prisoners of war. (1)

**9** Reds and Whites. (2)

**10** Any *two* from: Britain *or* France *or* Poland *or* USA *or* Japan *or* Finland. (2) This intervention turned many patriotic Russians against the Whites.

**11** The Reds could move supplies and troops rapidly. (1)
Trotsky could visit and encourage the Red Army. (1)

**12** All factories were taken over by the government. (1)
Peasants were forced to hand over surplus food. (1)
Rationing and work discipline were introduced. (1)

**13** The Russian economy improved. (1) Nepmen and kulaks became wealthy. (1) Some Communists opposed NEP as a retreat from revolution. (1) The risks of NEP led the Communists to ban factions and other parties temporarily. This was later used by Stalin to justify his one-party state.

TOTAL

## How did Stalin become leader?

- Before he died, Lenin's worries about Stalin led him to turn to Trotsky. Trotsky was popular with ordinary party members and the Red Army, but not with the other communist leaders.
- Many leaders, such as **Zinoviev**, **Kamenev**, **Bukharin** and especially **Stalin**, resented his earlier non-Bolshevik past and his sudden rise within the party after 1917.
- Before he died, Lenin wrote his **Testament** which listed the strengths and weaknesses of all the main Communists and ended with a recommendation that Stalin be dismissed from all positions of power.
- But Stalin used jealousies between the leaders, Trotsky's illness and his own position as General Secretary to stage-manage Lenin's funeral so that he appeared to have been very close to Lenin.
- More importantly, he persuaded the Communist leaders, who were all more popular than he was, not to act on Lenin's *Testament* and not to publish it, despite the protests of Lenin's widow.
- Zinoviev and Kamenev thought they could take over as the new leaders, using Stalin's control of party organisation. These three formed the **Triumvirate** to prevent Trotsky becoming leader.
- Lenin and the Bolsheviks had believed that only revolutions in more advanced countries could achieve Communism and that without these Russia couldn't even become socialist. After Lenin's death, Trotsky continued to believe in the idea of World Revolution and in **Permanent Revolution** which involved state industrialisation and state collective farms.
- Stalin countered this with a policy called **Socialism in One Country**. This said that though revolutions in other countries had failed, Russia could still build socialism by following Lenin's NEP.

- **The first stage** of Stalin's plan to become sole leader was to publish the earlier disagreement between Lenin and Trotsky. Using his control of the party appointments, the 1921 ban on factions and the jealousies and fears of other Communist leaders, Stalin persuaded the party to outvote Trotsky. In **1925**, Trotsky was **forced to resign** as Commissar for War, a potentially powerful position.
- **The second stage** of his plan was directed against his Triumvir partners, Zinoviev and Kamenev, who were becoming suspicious of Stalin's motives and policies.
- From 1925, while Zinoviev and Kamenev formed an alliance with Trotsky, the **Left Opposition**, Stalin and the Centre allied with Bukharin and the Right. They were divided over economic policy. Stalin and Bukharin wanted to continue with NEP, while Trotsky, Zinoviev and Kamenev argued for its end and a return to soviet and party democracy.
- Stalin again used his power as General Secretary, and the 1921 ban on factions, to manipulate party congress and elections to outvote his opponents. In 1927, Trotsky, Zinoviev, Kamenev and other left-wing communists **were expelled from the party**.
- In **the third stage** of his plan from 1928, Stalin turned on Bukharin and the Right. He used Trotsky's economic policies to oppose Bukharin, who continued to support NEP.
- Stalin used his party job to remove Bukharin's supporters from important positions. In desperation, Bukharin turned to Trotsky who had been exiled to Siberia in 1928.
- But it was too late. Bukharin was defeated and, in **1929**, **Trotsky** was **exiled from the Soviet Union**. Stalin was left as sole leader of the CPSU.

## Stalin and industry

- In 1928, Stalin decided to modernise Soviet industry rapidly which, despite the success of the NEP, was still largely undeveloped. Only 20 per cent of the population was employed in industry.
- Stalin decided to industrialise the country because:
  - he feared invasion by capitalist countries. They had sent armies to fight the Reds in the Civil War and since 1920 most had operated an economic blockade. Developed industry would make Russia stronger.
  - he believed the more prosperous peasants were deliberately reducing production to keep prices high. Rapid industrialisation would require dramatic changes in agriculture to feed a growing industrial and urban population. This would provide an opportunity to break the power of the kulaks and the nepmen.
- In 1928 Stalin began a **planned economy**. The State Planning Commission, **Gosplan**, drew up a **Five-Year Plan**. This set production increase targets for each industry.
- The **First Five-Year Plan (1928–32)** concentrated on **heavy industry** – coal, iron steel, oil, electricity. Successful industrialisation would need plenty of steel and energy.
- The **Second Five-Year Plan (1932–37)** continued the emphasis on heavy industry, but also focused on transport and mining.

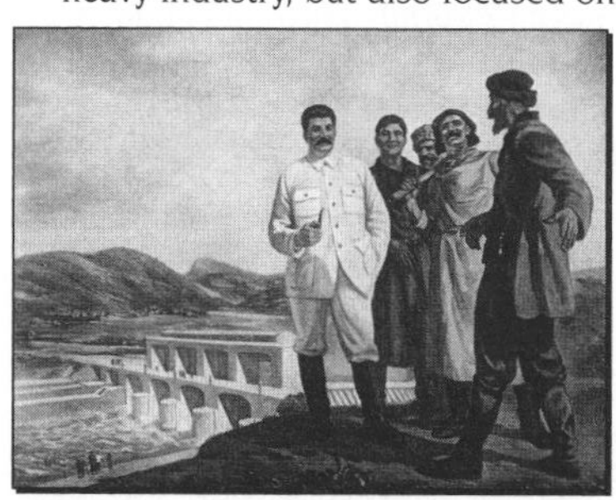

*Painting of Stalin talking with peasants and workers at a new dam*

- The **Third Five-Year Plan (1938 onwards)** put more emphasis on **light industry** and **consumer goods**, but had to be switched to war production, as the threat from Nazi Germany increased.
- Overall, these Five-Year Plans were very successful. Targets were often unrealistically high and so frequently were not achieved, but industrial production did increase dramatically.
- By 1941, the USSR was sufficiently industrialised to withstand and eventually defeat Hitler's invading armies.
- In addition new industries and new industrial towns and cities like Magnitogorsk were built.
- These huge increases were achieved in various ways:
  - **skilled foreign workers** who taught new skills
  - **women** were recruited to industry in large numbers
  - **peasants** were encouraged to work in factories
  - **forced labour** of prisoners
  - **Stakhanovism** 'super' workers were given extra pay and privileges for high output, their norms provided the base for rates of pay
  - **increased hours of work**
  - **strict work discipline**, for example fines for lateness
  - **government propaganda** which showed how hard work was making Russia and Communism stronger.
- Though the USSR quickly became a powerful industrial nation, 'real' wages generally fell, and there were great shortages of consumer goods because of the concentration on heavy industry. Also, housing was overcrowded in the industrial towns.
- However, **full employment** and **free health care and education** in the USSR contrasted with capitalist countries which suffered high unemployment and poverty during the Depression of the 1930s.

## Stalin and Russia (1–4)

**1** What seemingly unimportant Communist Party job did Stalin take on in 1922? (1)

**2** What document, written by Lenin just before his death, recommended that Stalin be removed from all his positions of power? (1)

**3** In what year did Lenin die? (1)

**4** Who, after Lenin, was the most well-known Communist leader? (1)

**5** Name *one* of the Communists who formed the Triumvirate with Stalin in order to prevent Trotsky from becoming the new leader? (1)

**6** What policy did Stalin put forward to oppose Trotsky's ideas of Permanent and World Revolution? (1)

**7** What important job was Trotsky forced to resign from in 1925? (1)

**8** Who was the leader of the right-wing Communists who, in the period 1925–27, supported Stalin in his struggle against left-wing Communists? (1)

**9** Name *one* of the two economic policies which Stalin developed from 1928 in his struggle against the right-wing of the Communist Party. (1)

**10** What percentage of the Soviet population worked in industry in 1928? (1)

**11** What were the *two* main motives behind Stalin's decision in 1928 to industrialise the Soviet Union as rapidly as possible? (2)

**12** How did Stalin set about trying to achieve a planned economy in industry? (2)

**13** What was Stakhanovism? (3)

**14** Name *three* other ways (apart from Stakhanovism) in which the government tried to ensure that the Five-Year Plans' targets were met? (3)

## ANSWERS & TUTORIALS

SCORE

**1** General Secretary of the Communist Party. (1) This meant Stalin could appoint his supporters to important positions.

**2** Lenin's *Testament*. (1)

**3** 1924 (1)

**4** Trotsky (1). He did not join the Bolsheviks until summer 1917. Those who had belonged since the 1903 spilt resented his rapid rise in the party.

**5** Zinoviev *or* Kamenev. (1)

**6** Socialism in One Country (1).

**7** Commissar for War (1). He was in charge of the Red Army, many soldiers supported him after the Civil War.

**8** Bukharin. (1)

**9** Forced collectivisation of agriculture *or* five-year plans for industrialisation. (1) Some left-wing Communists thought Stalin had accepted their ideas, and so gave him their support.

**10** 20 per cent. (1)

**11** Fear of invasion. (1) A desire to weaken the power of the kulaks. (1) Rapid industrialisation would need modernisation of agriculture which would give Stalin the opportunity to deal with the kulaks.

**12** A central State Planning Commission (Gosplan) (1) drew up production targets in Five-Year Plans. (1)

**13** Stakhanov was a coal miner who apparently dug a massive amount of coal in one shift. (1) Other 'super' workers were helped to achieve huge production figures. (1) These figures were used to make workers try to produce similar amounts. (1) Stakhanovites were treated as heroes and given privileges.

**14** Any *three* from: Recruiting skilled foreign workers *or* women to work in factories *or* peasants to leave the land *or* using forced labour *or* increasing the hours of work *or* harsher work discipline *or* government propaganda. (3)

TOTAL

## Stalin and collectivisation

- Stalin realised he needed to modernise Soviet agriculture to make the industrial Five-Year Plans work. Agriculture needed to:
  - **produce more food** for the growing industrial population.
  - **provide more workers** for the new factories. An efficient agriculture needs fewer farm workers.
  - **increase food exports** to enable the USSR to buy advanced foreign machinery.
- But Soviet agriculture was very backward with few machines, old-fashioned methods and many small, privately-owned farms. Most peasants had little or no land, but some, the **kulaks**, became wealthy under the NEP.
- Stalin's plan was to merge small peasant farms into a larger **state collective farm** called **kolkhoz**, which would be more efficient.
- To help these collective farms **Motor Tractor Stations (MTS)** provided tractors and other modern machinery.
- The peasants lost most of their land, much of which they had gained during and after the 1917 Revolutions. They were allowed to keep small plots of their own.
- Stalin tried to persuade peasants to join collectives voluntarily, but few did, so he resorted to **forced collectivisation**.

*'Come and join our kolkhoz, comrade!'*
*A government propaganda poster*

# STALIN AND RUSSIA (6)

- **Most opposition** to Stalin's forced collectivisation **came from the kulaks**. Many preferred to slaughter their animals and destroy their tools and crops rather than hand them over to the collectives.
- Stalin decided to take harsh measures to end this widespread opposition. Those who resisted were forced from their homes and settled in poor farming areas. Others were put into forced labour camps and many were executed.
- Not surprisingly, this greatly disrupted farming and peasants who remained were often reluctant to work enthusiastically on the collectives. The result was that **agricultural output was greatly reduced** (see table below), the opposite of what Stalin had planned:

**Agricultural output at the start of First Five-Year Plan (1928) and the second Five Year Plan (1933)**

| | 1928 | 1933 |
|---|---|---|
| Grain harvest | 73.3 million tonnes | 68.4 million tonnes |
| State grain demands | 10.8 million | 22.6 million tonnes |
| Numbers of cattle | 70.5 million | 38.4 million |
| Numbers of pigs | 26.0 milion | 12.1 million |

- The government sent armed detachments into the countryside to collect the food to avoid starvation in the industrial towns, just as **famine** hit many rural areas.
- But, even after the famine was over, Russian agriculture remained weak and inefficient for decades to come. Production figures began to exceed 1928 levels just before Germany invaded in 1941.

## Stalin's dictatorship

- By 1929, Stalin had removed all his main rivals from the Communist Party. He always feared new opponents, even some of his supporters had at first opposed his proposals to expel leading Communists.
- Stalin decided to establish a **totalitarian dictatorship** to make sure of his power. At first, he used the **secret police** (OGPU–NKVD) to arrest anyone even slightly critical of him.
- Stalin always felt insecure. **Kirov**, the party official in charge of Leningrad, seemed as popular as Stalin with delegates at the 17th Congress of the Communist Party in 1934. Soon after, Kirov was murdered. Stalin used this as an excuse to launch a **purge** of the Communist Party.
- Thousands of party officials were arrested. At a series of **show trials** in 1936, 1937 and 1938, they were accused of spying for the West or even for Nazi Germany. Zinoviev, Kamenev, Bukharin and Trotsky's supporters were all victims.
- By 1938, all the original Bolshevik leaders except Trotsky had either been executed or had committed suicide. Stalin also purged the Red Army commanders in 1937 and 1938: about a fifth of all officers were executed.
- Stalin now resorted to a campaign of **terror**. No one was safe from arrest, interrogation, imprisonment or execution. Many of the victims were sent to **forced labour camps**, where they were made to work on public schemes. Conditions were bad and food inadequate, so many died.

*'Stalin the Executioner alone remains.'*
*A poster made by Stalin's exiled opponents*

- Stalin also used **propaganda** and **censorship** to build up his dictatorship. Only the successes of his government were broadcast. The press, radio, cinema and the arts were all censored.

*A poster of Stalin, 1930s*

- Stalin also developed a **personality cult** to show himself as the true successor of Lenin. Statues and posters of Stalin appeared everywhere, and towns and streets were named after him.
- To gain the support of **young people**, Stalin ordered all history books to be re-written to show that he, not Trotsky or the other Communists, was the most important leader after Lenin. The Communist leaders of the 1920s were deleted from books and photographs, or were depicted as opponents of Lenin and agents of capitalist countries.
- Stalin also took control of the various youth movements. The leaders of **Komsomol** (Young Communist League) were carefully vetted before appointment.
- Stalin did also have much genuine support because there was:
  - **greater equality for women** who benefited from increased equality at work and from the crèches and nurseries provided by the state.
  - **free and improved health services**. By 1939 the USSR had more doctors per head of the population than Britain.
  - **free and improved education**. Much was done to improve literacy and to develop secondary education.
  - **improved living standards** after the early problems of the Five-Year Plans.
  - **improved leisure facilities**. Every factory and new town had cheap public transport, sports grounds, cinemas, swimming pools.

## Stalin and Russia (5–8)

**1** Give *one* reason why Stalin's plans to industrialise the Soviet Union needed great changes in agriculture. (1)

**2** What name was given to the richer peasants who had become wealthy under NEP? (1)

**3** What was a kolkhoz? (1)

**4** Mention *one* way in which kulaks showed their opposition to forced collectivisation. (1)

**5** What was the early result of forced collectivisation? (1)

**6** Why did the government send armed convoys into the countryside in the early 1930s? (1)

**7** What were the OGPU and NKVD? (1)

**8** Name the popular Communist party chief of Leningrad who was murdered in 1934. (1)

**9** What name is given to the mass arrest of Communists which Stalin launched after this murder? (1)

**10** Name *two* years in which important show trials took place. (2)

**11** Name *two* important 'Old Bolsheviks' (the 'Old Guard') who by 1938 were victims of these show trials. (2)

**12** What happened to Trotsky? (2)

**13** Apart from the secret police, purges and show trials, give *two* other ways in which Stalin built up his dictatorship. (2)

**14** Give *three* ways in which, under Stalin, people's lives changed for the better between 1928 and 1941. (3)

SCORE

**1** More food was needed for the increased town population *or* workers had to be moved from agriculture to industry *or* he wanted food for export to buy foreign machinery. (1) By 1928, agriculture was producing less food than was needed. Changes would increase his control of the countryside.

**2** Kulaks. (1)

**3** A state collective farm. (1)

**4** Any *one* from: Refused to hand over their farms *or* slaughtered their animals *or* destroyed their tools and crops. (1)

**5** Food production fell considerably. (1) The famine Stalin feared before 1928 came in 1932–33.

**6** To ensure that factory workers did not starve. (1)

**7** Different names given to the secret police. (1)

**8** Kirov. (1)

**9** A purge. (1)

**10** Any *two* from: 1936 *or* 1937 *or* 1938. (2)

**11** Any *two* from: Zinoviev *or* Kamenev *or* Bukharin. (2)

**12** He had been exiled, so was found guilty in his absence. (1) He was murdered in Mexico in 1940, on Stalin's orders. (1)

**13** Any *two* from: Propaganda *or* censorship *or* development of a 'personality cult' *or* control of communist youth movements *or* use of labour camps. (2)

**14** Any *three* from: Greater equality for women *or* improved health services *or* improved education *or* improving living standards *or* improved leisure facilities. (3) Living standards were considerably lower than in Britain, but ordinary Russians felt themselves better off than before 1917. Many were proud of the achievements of the Five-Year Plans.

TOTAL

## Isolationism

- Woodrow Wilson, the Democrat President who took the USA into the First World War and drew up the Fourteen Points as a basis for peace, wanted the USA to continue its involvement in Europe.
- But many Americans wanted the USA to return to its traditional policy of **isolationism**. This meant:
  - staying out of foreign alliances
  - not playing much part in European affairs.
- In 1919, the majority of Americans saw Europe as:
  - the 'Old World' from which many of them had migrated to escape poverty and oppression.
  - a place full of dangerous revolutionary ideas like socialism, Communism, anarchism and the frightening revolutions which had broken out between 1917 and 1920.
  - the reason for the deaths of 100,000 US soldiers who fought in the First World War.
- Isolationism led the Senate, one of the two Houses of the US Congress and dominated by the Republicans since 1918, to reject the Treaty of Versailles. This meant the US refused to join the League of Nations.
- The USA also placed increasing restrictions on immigration and trade, especially from south and eastern Europe. Many of these people were Catholics and some were socialists, Communists or anarchists. Most immigrants before 1900 were from north and western Europe, known as **WASP**s (White Anglo-Saxon Protestants). The new restrictions included:
  - 1917 a literacy test for all immigrants
  - 1921 a limit on immigrants and a quota system.
  - 1922 the Fordney–McCumber Act which put high **tariffs** (import duties) on foreign goods.

## Prosperity in the USA in the 1920s

- After the First World War, the US economy in the 1920s **boomed**. There was a great increase in production, especially of **consumer goods**.
- This boom was based on several factors:
  - The USA had plenty of **raw materials** (coal, iron, oil).
  - During most of the First World War, the USA stayed out of the fighting. It supplied weapons and food to European countries, and took over selling goods to the colonial markets previously supplied by Britain, France and Germany. The war allowed the US chemical industry to take the lead over the German chemical industry.
  - Profits made by US investors and bankers during the war meant they could invest in new industries in the USA.
  - Tariffs protected US industries from foreign competition.
  - New technology (electricity, telephone, radio) was successful. Some new industries, like car building, led to growth in supplying industries, like leather, rubber and steel.
  - The sale of consumer goods was helped by new techniques of **advertising**, and by the spread of **hire purchase** as a way of buying.
- The Republican presidents of the 1920s ended Wilson's restrictions on industry and commerce to protect the public. They believed in **laissez-faire**, which kept taxes low and left business and industry alone.
- Not all Americans shared in this prosperity of the 1920s:
  - **Farmers** faced competition from European farmers and problems caused by tariffs and over-production.
  - **The poor** Nearly half the population lived below the poverty line. These people were unemployed; worked in old or declining industries; or were unskilled or casual workers.

## The Roaring Twenties

- Life in the USA during the 1920s could be symbolised by its huge cities with **skyscrapers**, lots of cars and lorries, chain stores and department stores, and cinemas, clubs and bars (the **Jazz Age**).
- In the 1920s, for the first time, the majority of people lived in cities and towns. The rural areas largely missed out on the 1920s prosperity. The 1920s affected people in different ways:
- **Black Americans**
  - In 1920, there were 12 million black Americans, three-quarters of whom lived in the South. They were freed from slavery in 1865, but they still suffered from poverty and discrimination, for example the '**Jim Crow**' laws prevented black people from voting.
  - There was **segregation** in the South between black and white people in schools, restaurants, transport and parks.
  - Black people suffered violence from the **Ku Klux Klan** (**KKK**), which increased its membership to five million by 1925. Many law officials in the rural south were sympathetic to the KKK, some were even members.

*Members of the Ku Klux Klan*

  - During the 1920s one and a half million black Americans left the South for the cities of the north where there were better chances of employment and education and no segregation. But there was still discrimination in jobs, wages and housing, and racial hostility in some areas.

- **Women**
  - The First World War meant American women worked in factories in large numbers.
  - In 1920, all women were given the vote. Divorce was made easier.
  - Some women, like the **Flappers**, enjoyed more social freedoms. Other areas of life, like politics, were not equally open and women's pay remained lower than men's.
- Not everyone in the USA shared the prosperity of the Roaring Twenties, it was also a time of social problems.
- **Prohibition**
  - In 1919 pressure from the women in the Anti-Saloon League and the Women's Christian Temperance Union resulted in the **Eighteenth Amendment** to the US Constitution. This made the sale, manufacture or transport of alcohol illegal. The **Volstead Act** made buying alcohol illegal.
  - Many people were prepared to break the law to drink alcohol. Speakeasies (illegal bars), moonshine (illegally made alcohol) and bootlegging (smuggling alcohol) were the result.
  - The Prohibitionists intended to improve life, instead many ordinary US citizens became criminals. Big-time **gangsters**, like Al Capone, became wealthy and powerful, able to bribe judges, police chiefs. The **Twenty-First Amendment** ended Prohibition in 1933.
- **Intolerance**
  - Powerful Americans, opposed to left-wing ideas, began a '**Red Scare**', in which **Socialists**, **Communists** and **Anarchists** were harassed by the police, and even deported from the USA. Many industrialists, such as Henry Ford, refused to allow people to join trade unions, often using violence against trade unionists. Trade-union membership in the 1920s dropped from five million to three million.
  - The main victims of **racism** in the 1920s were black Americans. Roman Catholics, Jews and foreigners also suffered.

## The USA, 1919–1941 (1–4)

1 Which American political party is associated with the policy of isolationism after the First World War? (1)

2 Name *one* of the European political ideologies which many Americans increasingly feared after 1917. (1)

3 What do the initials WASP stand for? (1)

4 How did the quota system of the 1921 Immigration Act work? (1)

5 Name *one* of the Republican Presidents between 1920 and 1933. (1)

6 Explain, briefly, what the Republican economic policy of *laissez-faire* meant in practical terms. (1)

7 Name *one* industry which benefited from the growing car industry during the economic boom of the 1920s. (1)

8 Identify *one* group of Americans who did not share in the increased prosperity of the 1920s. (1)

9 Which white racist organisation wore white sheets with pointed hoods? (1)

10 Where in the USA was this group most active? (1)

11 How was Prohibition achieved in the USA in 1919? (2)

12 What were speakeasies; moonshine; bootlegging? (3)

13 What were the main problems of Prohibition? (3)

14 Who were the two Italian anarchists executed in 1927 during the 'Red Scare'? (2)

*Government officials destroying cases of beer during Prohibition*

## ANSWERS & TUTORIALS

SCORE

1. The Republicans. (1) Isolationism only related to Europe not to Latin America and the Pacific.
2. Any *one* from: Socialism, Communism *or* Anarchism. (1)
3. White Anglo-Saxon Protestant. (1) Descendants of immigrants from north and west Europe, who despised the recent immigrants from the poorer south and east of Europe.
4. Immigrants were limited to the proportion of people from that country already in the USA. (1) This greatly reduced the numbers of 'new' immigrants.
5. Any *one* from: Harding, Coolidge *or* Hoover. (1)
6. Leaving industry and business alone, with no government interference or restrictions. (1)
7. Any *one* from: plate glass, leather, rubber, steel, oil and petrol or road-building. (1) Industry expanded when the assembly line was introduced.
8. Any *one* from: farmers, the poor *or* black Americans. (1) Farmers faced competition from abroad and tariffs on US food. Machines replaced people.
9. The Ku Klux Klan. (1)
10. The South. (1) The majority of black Americans lived there as did many poor whites.
11. Many women believed alcohol damaged family life and campaigned for it to be banned. (1) Alcohol was banned under the Eighteenth Amendment and the Volstead Act. (1)
12. Illegal bars; illegally-made alcohol; smuggling alcohol into the USA. (3)
13. Ordinary citizens became minor criminals. (1) Crime syndicates and gangsters thrived. (1) It cost the government large amounts of money to enforce. (1)
14. Sacco (1). Vanzetti (1). Witnesses said they were not at the scene of the crime, but the judge and jury were biased because they were anarchists.

TOTAL

## The Wall Street Crash and the Great Depression

- By the end of the 1920s, the US economy faced a crisis of **over-production**. This was because:
  - nearly half the population could not afford consumer goods
  - the richest people had already bought all they needed
  - US industry could not sell abroad because other countries had put tariffs on US goods.
- This situation was made more dangerous by a **boom in shares**. The number of people with shares rose from four million in 1920 to twenty million by 1929. Many people, known as speculators, bought their shares '**on the margin**', only part-paying for them, hoping to pay the rest when they sold them at a profit. Others, by illegal evasion known as 'skulduggery', controlled the majority of shares in many companies.
- In the autumn of 1929, some investors lost confidence in the boom, because of fears about overproduction, and began to sell shares. This triggered panic selling of millions of shares. Prices fell rapidly.
- This was the **Wall Street Crash**. On 24 October, 'Black Thursday', thirteen million shares were sold, 29 October was worse with sixteen million sold. The situation was made worse because banks, who had lent money to speculators to buy shares, needed to cover their loans and so rushed to sell their shares.
- The effects of the Wall Street Crash were dramatic:
  - Those who had invested in shares were ruined; many were bankrupted.
  - Many smaller banks went broke and thousands of people lost their savings.
  - Many companies closed and their workers became unemployed.
  - As people lost confidence and their jobs, sales fell, and so more people became unemployed.

- This led to the **Great Depression**. By 1933, the worst year, industrial production had dropped by 40 per cent; share prices by 80 per cent; and unemployment had risen to 14 million. The US economy seemed locked into a downward spiral.
- The Great Depression hit farmers hard. Prices fell, so they could not keep up mortgage repayments to the banks and had to sell their farms. In the Mid-West soil erosion resulted in the '**Dust Bowl**': the soil blew away and the land could not be farmed.
- The Republican belief in ***laissez-faire*** and '**rugged individualism**' meant there was no system of unemployment benefit. In the cities, hard-hit people depended entirely on soup kitchens and hand-outs.

*Unemployed people in New York queuing for bread, 1930*

- President Hoover clung to his belief in *laissez-faire* and so did little to help, believing that business would improve and that 'prosperity is just around the corner'.
- The unemployed and homeless lived in cardboard shacks which they called '**Hoovervilles**'. The '**Bonus Army**', of former soldiers asking for their war pension to be paid early, camped outside the White House. In 1932, Hoover signed an Emergency Relief and Reconstruction Act, but it was too little, too late.

## Roosevelt and the New Deal

- In the 1932 Presidential elections, Hoover was opposed by the Democrat **Franklin Delano Roosevelt**. He believed that the government should spend money to help the US economy. He had no firm policies, but he promised the American people a **New Deal**.
- Roosevelt and the Democrats won the November elections easily. In his **First Hundred Days**, Roosevelt set up new government agencies to carry out his aims:
  - Emergency Banking Act
  - Federal Emergency Relief Agency (**FERA**)
  - Civilian Conservation Corps (**CCC**)
  - National Industrial Recovery Act (**NIRA**)
    Part 1 set up the Public Works Authority (**PWA**)
    Part 2 set up the '**Blue Eagle**' scheme
  - Farm Credit Association (**FCA**)
  - Home Owners Loan Corporation (**HOLC**)
  - Tennessee Valley Authority (**TVA**).

  These are often known as the **Alphabet Agencies**.

*Dam built by the Tennessee Valley Authority*

- Roosevelt's ideas and policies were opposed by:
  - **conservatives** and **industrialists** who disliked government intervention in business, calling the New Deal a form of socialism.
  - **radicals** who felt it did not do enough for the poor.
  - the **Supreme Court**, whose judges often ruled New Deal laws illegal, for example the NIRA in 1935 and the AAA in 1936. They argued that federal (national) government did not have the right to say what each state should do.
- Despite this opposition, Roosevelt's first attempts to deal with the problems of the Great Depression, and his ability to communicate with people through his use of the radio for '**fireside chats**', resulted in a massive win for him in the 1936 elections.
- Roosevelt's **Second New Deal** began in 1935. It included:
  - The Wagner Act
  - Social Security Act
  - Works Progress Administration (**WPA**)

  In addition, he re-introduced some of the First New Deal laws rejected by the Supreme Court.
- Problems and opposition continued.
  - By 1937, consumer spending was only 75 per cent of what it had been in 1929.
  - New Deal policies failed to end unemployment. It was 9.5 million at the start of the Second World War in 1939. War production began to lower unemployment.
  - The destruction of surplus food and animals to help farmers made food too expensive for many poor people.
  - New Deal laws allowed women and black Americans to be paid less than white men; while AAA quotas led to millions of poor black farmers being pushed off the land.
- Roosevelt remained popular with the voters, and went on to win the 1940 and the 1944 Presidential elections.

## The USA, 1919–1941 (5–8)

**1** What is meant by 'over-production crisis'? (1)

**2** What was the Fordney–McCumber Act of 1922? (1)

**3** What does buying shares 'on the margin' mean? (1)

**4** Where are shares bought and sold in the USA? (1)

**5** What happened to US share prices in October 1929? (1)

**6** Why did 24 October 1929 become known as 'Black Thursday'? (1)

**7** How did people paying for goods in instalments contribute to the downward economic spiral after the Wall Street Crash? (1)

**8** What was the 'dust-bowl' which hit parts of the Mid-West during the Great Depression? (1)

**9** Who were the 'Okies' and the 'Arkies'? (2)

**10** What were President Hoover's two main beliefs during the first years of the Great Depression. (2)

*A farmworker's shack during the Depression*

**11** Who won the 1932 US Presidential elections and what political party did he lead? (2)

**12** What are the full names of the 'alphabet agencies' known by the initials AAA and NIRA? (2)

**13** What was the reaction of the Supreme Court towards New Deal policies? (2)

**14** Why was a Second New Deal started in 1935? (2)

# ANSWERS & TUTORIALS

SCORE

**1** An industry or a country produces more than it can sell. (1) This happened in the US, where the 1920s boom was based on selling more and more consumer goods.
**2** It placed high tariffs (import duties) on foreign goods. (1) These were increased in 1930. Other countries then did the same, so reducing US goods sold abroad.
**3** Buying shares by only paying a 10 per cent deposit. (1) The rest was to be paid after selling the shares at a profit.
**4** The New York Stock Exchange on Wall Street. (1)

**5** They fell dramatically. (1) Some speculators sold shares which triggered panic selling.
**6** Thirteen million shares were sold in one day at low prices. (1) 29 October was worse. Sixteen million shares were sold and shareholders lost $8 billion.
**7** People who lost their jobs could not keep up their repayments, so their goods were re-possessed. (1)
**8** Over-farming led to serious soil erosion, the topsoil just blew away. (1)
**9** Farmers forced to leave their farms because of the dust-bowl and lack of money. (1) The 'Okies' were from Oklahoma, and the 'Arkies' from Arkansas. (1) The worst year was 1934.

**10** *Laissez-faire*. (1) Rugged Individualism. (1) He believed 'prosperity was just around the corner'.
**11** Roosevelt. (1) Democrats. (1)
**12** Agricultural Adjustment Administration. (1) National Industrial Recovery Act. (1) AAA helped farmers by increasing food prices; NIRA provided jobs.
**13** Many judges were conservative and disagreed with Roosevelt's laws. (1) They used their power to block many New Deal laws as being unconstitutional. (1) The Supreme Court ruled against eleven out of sixteen alphabet agencies.
**14** First New Deal laws were blocked by the Supreme Court. (1) Unemployment and poverty continued. (1) A new depression began in 1937 caused by a decline in world trade and Roosevelt's decision to reduce federal government spending.

TOTAL

## How was the League of Nations set up?

- A League of Nations was proposed by President Woodrow Wilson, to prevent war. It was the last of his **Fourteen Points,** 1918.
- The League's membership, powers and aims were decided during the peace negotiations at Versailles with Britain and France. Its headquarters were in Geneva.
- It was agreed that it should be a '**parliament of nations**' which would
  - solve disputes by **negotiation**.
  - encourage **disarmament**.
  - try to improve health, education, living and working conditions for people all over the world. Poverty and injustice were seen as important causes of war.
- The League would try to end violence of aggressive states by:
  - **pressure** of world opinion;
  - **sanctions** (trade bans) applied by all members
  - **force**, but only as a last resort.
- But, there were problems:
  - The USA, Germany and Russia were not members.
  - Britain's interest in its empire, and France's wish to ensure the suppression of Germany, meant they did not always cooperate.
  - Britain and France, the victors, dominated the League, so the defeated countries had little respect for it
  - White European nations dominated the League.

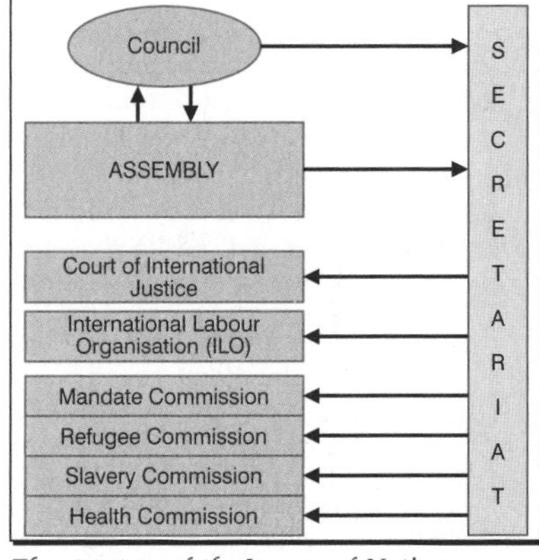


*The structure of the League of Nations*

## Was the League successful in the 1920s?

- In the 1920s, the League of Nations achieved several **successes**:
  - helping refugees from the First World War return home.
  - reducing diseases worldwide through its Health Committee.
  - helping stop slave labour and the use of dangerous chemicals.
- The League settled several border disputes:
  - **1921** **Upper Silesia** between Poland and Germany<br>**Åaland Islands** between Finland and Sweden
  - **1925** **Greek invasion of Bulgaria**
- It also had failures:
  - **1920** **Vilna** between Poland and Finland
  - **1920–22** **Treaty of Sèvres** between Turkey and Greece
  - **1923** **The Ruhr** occupied by France and Belgium without reference to the League<br>**Corfu** between Italy and Greece

  Poland, Turkey, France and Italy used **aggression** to achieve their aims.
- The attempts to achieve **peace** had mixed results:
  - **1922** **Washington Treaty** USA, Britain, France, Japan and Italy agreed to limit naval expansion for ten years.
  - **1923** Proposals for a **disarmament treaty** were blocked by Britain
  - **1925** **Locarno Pact** Germany accepted its western borders, as in the Treaty of Versailles, admitted there should be discussions about its eastern borders
  - **1926** **Germany allowed to join the League**
  - **1928** **Kellogg–Briand Pact** over 45 countries agreed never to go to war
- Under the Dawes Plan, 1924, Germany was able to pay some reparations to the Allies.
- Some problems remained:
  - **Germany** was still resentful of the Treaty of Versailles, though by 1928 its economy was doing well.
  - **France** was still fearful of Germany.
  - **Poland** and **Czechoslovakia** had disputed borders.

## Was the League successful in the 1930s?

- Despite some successes in the 1920s, the League had not established itself as the main way of settling disputes. Its leading members, Britain and France, often followed their own policies.
- These weaknesses were made worse when the **Great Depression** hit the world in the 1930s.
- Extreme nationalist governments came to power in many countries. They often followed an **aggressive foreign policy** to cover up economic problems at home. Italy, Germany and Japan all did this.
- Other countries tended to put their own economic interests first. They did not impose economic sanctions on an aggressor if that ban could harm their own trade.
- These problems can be seen in several serious crises and conflicts before the Second World War.
  - **1931 Manchuria**
    When **Japan**, a League member, invaded Manchuria in northern China, Japan's civilian government tried to stop their army. The generals carried on and by 1932 all Manchuria was occupied. The League took a year to produce the **Lytton Report** which criticised Japan and imposed sanctions, so Japan left the League in 1933.

The Doormat, *a cartoon of 1931. The Japanese soldier has trodden on the 'Honour of the League'; the elderly man is using a 'face-saving outfit' on the woman who represents the League.*

- **1932–33 Disarmament Conference**
  This attempted to continue the work of 1923. It failed as in 1933 Hitler became Chancellor of Germany and began to re-arm. Later that year, he took Germany out of the League. As the Depression hit, many countries began to re-arm, sometimes as a way of providing employment and stopping industrial decline.
- **1935 Abyssinia**
  Mussolini, the fascist dictator of Italy, decided to invade Abyssinia to gain popularity and to counter the effects of the Depression. Haile Selassie, emperor of Abyssinia, appealed to the League but Britain and France would not take action against Italy. They had allied with Italy, in the **Stresa Front**, to curb Nazi Germany. Britain and France secretly drew up the **Hoare–Laval Plan** which would give Mussolini most of Abyssinia. Public protest led to sanctions, but these did not include oil or coal.
- From 1935 onwards the League appeared increasingly weak and the failure of disarmament ever more apparent. The secret Anglo–German Naval Treaty, 1935, added to this failure.
- By the mid-1930s, many felt the League had failed. Its main problems were:
  - the absence of the powerful USA and, until 1934, the USSR. As non-members, they could and did trade with countries facing League sanctions.
  - Being too closely linked to the victors of the First World War and the peace treaties.
  - The lack of unity between Britain and France.
  - Difficulties with sanctions, especially during the Depression.
  - No armed forces to impose decisions.
  - Slow to make decisions.
  - The rise of powerful nationalist dictators and militaristic governments prepared to ignore the League and to use force.

## International relations (1–4)

1. Who was the US President who proposed a League of Nations in 1918? (1)
2. Which country, apart from Britain, France and Italy, was the fourth permanent member of the League of Nations Council? (1)
3. Which powerful country never joined the League of Nations? (1)
4. Britain was more concerned about its Empire and trade. What was France's main concern after 1918? (1)
5. What organisation, separate from the League, did Britain and France set up in 1919? (1)
6. Name *one* failure of the League to deal with aggression in 1923? (1)
7. What success did the League have in dealing with aggression in 1925? (1)
8. When was the Locarno Pact signed? (1)
9. Why was Japan criticised by the League's Lytton Committee Report of 1932, and what was Japan's reaction? (2)
10. Why did the Disarmament Conference of 1932–33 end in failure? (2)
11. What *two* developments in 1935 seriously undermined the Stresa Front between Britain, France and Italy? (2)
12. Why did Mussolini decide to invade Abyssinia in 1935? (3)
13. Name the *three* important countries whose non-membership of the League, between 1919 and 1935, severely weakened its effectiveness. (3)

SCORE

**1** Woodrow Wilson. (1)

**2** Japan. (1)

**3** USA. (1) It was President Wilson's idea, but the Republicans won control of the Senate and the US returned to a policy of isolationism towards Europe.

**4** Keeping Germany weak. (1) These different interests meant Britain and France often acted independently of each other and of the League. France was never sure of British support.

**5** The Conference of Ambassadors. (1) Set up to enforce the Treaty of Versailles before the League was established.

**6** *Either* the French occupation of the Ruhr *or* the Italian occupation of Corfu. (1)

**7** The Greek invasion of Bulgaria. (1) The League condemned Greece which withdrew its troops.

**8** 1925 (1) Germany was allowed to join the League in 1926.

**9** It had invaded Manchuria in 1931. (1) Japan simply left the League in 1933. (1)

**10** The countries could not agree. (1) Hitler decided to withdraw Germany and to re-arm. (1) The main problem was whether to disarm to Germany's level or to allow Germany to re-arm to other countries' levels.

**11** Britain and France's support of limited League sanctions against Italy after its invasion of Abyssinia. (1) Britain's signing the Anglo–German Naval Treaty. (1)

**12** To increase his popularity by winning a quick victory. (1) To solve economic problems caused by the Depression. (1) To avenge an earlier defeat in 1896. (1).

**13** The USA. (1) Germany. (1) Soviet Union. (1). Germany was a member from 1926 to 1933, the Soviet Union was not allowed to join until 1934. The USA and the USSR, as non-members, ignored League sanctions and had important trade links with Japan.

TOTAL

## Hitler and the causes of the Second World War

- As early as 1924, Hitler outlined plans in *Mein Kampf* which would obviously involve war:
  - **All German-speakers should be united** in the same country. This was against the terms of the Treaty of Versailles.
  - **Germany should have more land**, taken from east European countries, especially the Soviet Union.
- Hitler realised these plans would mean war. He said Germany should ignore the Treaty of Versailles and **re-arm**.
- As soon as he became Chancellor of Germany in 1933:
  - Hitler began to re-arm and to increase the size of Germany's armed forces. This was done partly to solve the problem of unemployment.
  - The German economy was put on a war footing.
  - The Hitler Youth was used to prepare young men for war.
- Hitler took other action in his first two years as Chancellor, 1933–35, which show how he was thinking:
  - **1933** Germany left the Disarmament Conference and the League of Nations.
  - **1934** Attempt to take over Austria by encouraging Austrian Nazis to cause distubances. This action was blocked by Mussolini's Italy, working through the **Stresa Front** formed in 1935 with Britain and France.
  - **1935** The **Saar** voted to rejoin Germany. Hitler openly began German re-armament, especially the airforce and army, although this was forbidden under the Treaty of Versailles. He built up the German navy following the secret Anglo–German Naval Agreement.
- Hitler also noted how **Japan's** invasion of Manchuria in 1931 and **Italy's** invasion of Abyssinia in 1935 had been ignored by the League of Nations, and that they had not suffered any serious penalties.

- Hitler became even bolder after 1935:
  - **1936** In March, Hitler ordered German troops to **re-occupy the Rhineland**, a de-militarised zone since the Treaty of Versailles. He was gambling that Britain and France would do nothing,
  - In November Hitler persuaded Italy to leave the Stresa Front and to sign the **Rome–Berlin Axis** with Nazi Germany.
  - **1937** Hitler and his new ally, Mussolini, decided to support the right-wing Nationalists in the **Spanish Civil War** despite the League of Nations' Non-Intervention policy. This was an opportunity to test German weapons and aircraft.
  - Germany, Italy and Japan signed the **Anti-Comintern Pact** against the Soviet Union so forming the Rome–Berlin–Tokyo Axis.
  - **1938** In March, in defiance of the Treaty of Versailles forbidding **Anschluss**, or union, between Germany and Austria, Hitler ordered the takeover of Austria. Britain and France did nothing.
  - In April, encouraged by his success so far, Hitler began to threaten the **Sudeten** border-area of **Czechoslovakia** where three million German-speakers lived.

*Map of Czechoslovakia showing border areas where German speakers lived.*

## Appeasement

- The British and French policy of **appeasement** began in the 1930s. It involved trying to keep Mussolini, and later Hitler, happy by agreeing to most of their territorial demands. This included '**revising**' the Treaty of Versailles, which Britain now saw as unfair.
- This policy of appeasement explains why Britain and France did little to oppose German and Italian aggression after 1933. It can be seen most clearly in the **Sudetenland Crisis** which lasted from April to September 1938.
  - The Sudetenland, previously part of the Habsburg Empire, had been given to the new state of Czechoslovakia. Three million German speakers lived there. With Hitler's encouragement, Henlein, the local Nazi party leader, complained that the German-speaking minority was being unfairly treated by the Czech government.
  - Hitler threatened to invade Czechoslovakia to 'protect' these **Sudeten Germans**, even though France had signed a treaty promising to protect Czechoslovakia.
  - In September, the British Prime Minister, **Chamberlain**, flew three times to meet Hitler to try to resolve the crisis. Hitler kept increasing his demands but finally, at the **Munich Conference**, Britain, France and Italy agreed to Hitler's demands that the Sudetenland be handed over to Germany.
  - The Czechs were furious. They had not been consulted and were forced to give up their border area which contained many of their defences.
  - The Russians were suspicious. They had offered to assist Czechoslovakia, but they had not been consulted either.

# INTERNATIONAL RELATIONS (8)

- After the Munich Conference, Hitler sent German troops to occupy the Sudetenland.
- His demands did not end. He made further threats against Czechoslovakia and in **March 1939**, German troops invaded the rest of Czechoslovakia. Again, Britain and France did nothing to oppose this Nazi aggression.
- Hitler interpreted this continued lack of opposition to mean that Britain and France would never oppose his aggressive foreign policy, provided he left Germany's western borders as established by the Treaty of Versailles.
- The British government assumed that **Poland** would be Hitler's next target. Britain signed an alliance with Poland.

*A Czech woman watches German forces march into Prague, 1939.*

- In August 1939, the Soviet Union signed the **Non-Aggression Pact** with Nazi Germany. Stalin was convinced that Hitler would eventually attack, and was suspicious about Britain's and France's refusal to make an anti-Nazi alliance with USSR. He decided to buy time to prepare the Soviet Union for war, using eastern Poland as a buffer zone.
- Historians have argued whether appeasement was a wise policy. Some see it as making war more likely as it encouraged Hitler to think he could do anything. Others see it as practical because Britain was not ready for war in 1938, and needed time to re-arm.
- When Hitler ordered the invasion of Poland in **September 1939**, Britain and France honoured their treaty with Poland, and declared war on Germany. The Second World War had begun.

## International relations (5–8)

**1** What was the title of the book, written in 1924, in which Hitler gave an early indication of his determination to break the Treaty of Versailles? (1)

**2** When did Hitler take Germany out of the Disarmament Conference and the League of Nations? (1)

**3** Which country did Hitler attempt to take over in 1934? (1)

**4** What was the main reason for the failure of this attempt? (1)

**5** What important agreement did Hitler sign with Britain in 1935? (1)

**6** What serious breach of the Treaty of Versailles did Hitler successfully achieve in March 1936? (1)

**7** What new agreement did Hitler sign in November 1936? (1)

**8** What was the 1937 document which suggests that Hitler told the German generals to be ready for war in five years time? (1)

**9** Which country was taken over by Nazi Germany in March 1938, and what is the name usually given to this takeover? (2)

**10** Why did Hitler feel quite confident that this takeover would be successful? (2)

**11** Give *two* reasons why, by September 1938, Hitler had decided he needed to take the part of Czechoslovakia known as Sudetenland? (2)

**12** What were the *three* main reasons for the policy of appeasement? (3)

**13** What were the consequences of the decision of the Munich Conference, in September 1938, to allow Nazi Germany to occupy the Sudetenland? (3)

# ANSWERS & TUTORIALS

SCORE

**1** *Mein Kampf or* My Struggle.(1)

**2** 1933. (1)

**3** Austria. (1)

**4** Germany was opposed by Italy, Britain and France. (1) This led to the formation of the Stresa Front, an agreement to oppose Nazi expansion.

**5** Anglo–German Naval Agreement. (1) This allowed Germany to build its navy up to 35 per cent of the size of the British navy.

**6** Re-militarisation of the Rhineland. (1)

**7** Rome–Berlin Axis. (1) By then, Italy had left the Stresa Front because of British and French criticism of its invasion of Abyssinia.

**8** Hossbach Memorandum. (1) This supports the claim that Hitler was planning for war from the beginning.

**9** Austria (1) Anschluss. (1)

**10** Any *two* from: Italy was now an ally (1) Britain and France had done nothing to oppose Japanese or Italian aggression (1). The German army was stronger after three years of re-armament (1).

**11** Any *two* from: To unite the Sudeten Germans with Germany *or* to win Czechoslovakia's border defences *or* to have the Skoda armaments works. (2)

**12** Horror of a war like the First World War. (1) Fear of high civilian casualties from air-raids. (1) Britain was not ready for war in 1938. (1) Also: recognition that the Treaty of Versailles had been too harsh or Germany was seen as a useful block against the USSR.

**13** Hitler was convinced that Britain and France would never oppose his expansion plans. (1) The conquest of the rest of Czechoslovakia was made easier. (1) Stalin was afraid that Britain and France were encouraging Hitler to attack the Soviet Union. (1) Moscow could now be reached by German bombers.

TOTAL

## The roots of apartheid

- **Race** has always been important in South Africa. The first people to live in the **Cape** area were black Africans. They were mainly herdsmen who moved over areas they did not own, but had traditionally been grazed by them.
- In the seventeenth century, mainly Dutch, white Europeans began to move into this area. These Dutch farmers, called **Boers**, took land from the Africans, often killing them or making them slaves. They created farms which prevented the movement of the Africans' animals. The Boers soon lost contact with Europe and developed their own language, **Afrikaans**. The Protestant Dutch Reformed Church stressed their racial superiority.
- During the wars with Napoleon's France, the Dutch colony in the Cape was taken over by Britain in 1805. From 1860, Britain set up sugar plantations in **Natal**, bringing in workers from India.
- The Boers disliked British rule, so from 1835 they started to leave the Cape in the **Great Trek**. By 1854, they had set up two new independent Boer republics, the **Transvaal** and the **Orange Free State**.
- **Diamonds** were discovered in the Orange Free State in 1867 and **gold** in the Transvaal in 1871. The Boers were not interested, so the mining industries soon came under British ownership, led by Cecil Rhodes. **The Boer War, 1899–1902**, ended with the defeat of the Boers by the British. The two Boer republics became part of the **Union of South Africa**, a colony of the British Empire.
- Britain had promised political rights to non-whites if the Boers were defeated, but these promises were not kept. The new government passed **segregationist laws** in line with Afrikaner views and, when unemployment rose in the 1920s and 1930s, it sacked blacks and restricted many jobs to whites.

## Apartheid begins

- After the Boer War, the Afrikaners tried to keep a separate identity and demanded tougher segregationist laws.
- In 1924, General Herzog, leader of the Nationalist Party, became Prime Minister. He restored the use of Afrikaans and passed segregationist laws.
- In the 1930s, an Afrikaner, **Dr Malan** founded the **(Purified) National Party** for Afrikaner control of South Africa. He became Prime Minister in 1948. Only whites (although they were only 12 per cent of the population), and some Coloureds in the Cape, had the vote. He was also supported by the Dutch Reformed Church and the **Broederbond**.
- The National Party's popularity with whites was mainly due to Malan's policy of **apartheid**, or apartness, which promimsed a stricter separation of blacks from whites.
- As soon as he became Prime Minister, Malan put his apartheid beliefs into practice:
  - **1950 Population Registration Act** classified the population into four categories.
  - **1952 Abolition of Passes Act** increased the use of passes for blacks.
  - **1953 Separate Amenities Act** segregated public facilities.
  - **1953 Bantu Education Act** restricted education for blacks.
  - **1956 Separate Representation of Voters Act** deprived Cape Coloureds of the vote.
- In 1958, **Verwoerd** became Prime Minister. He also supported strict apartheid and began a second phase of apartheid legislation. The **Bantu Self-Government Act 1959** set up eight separate Bantu homelands or '**Bantustans**'.

## Resistance to apartheid

- There was resistance to the strict enforcement of racial segregation and white 'supremacy', so South Africa soon became a police state.
- Before apartheid, Africans had tried to resist the Boer, and then the British, conquest of South Africa. In 1912, some Africans formed the South African Native National Congress to oppose the growth of segregation. In 1923, this became the **African National Congress**, but it failed to stop any of the racist laws of the 1920s and 1930s because:
  - Each tribe was a nation and were unused to co-operation.
  - White governments made sure there were few educated Africans who could become leaders.
  - The mainly middle-class **ANC** was suspicious of the **South African Communist Party**, set up in 1921, which was the main white anti-racist group.
  - Police violence and the British government's refusal to help meant the ANC had no success before the 1940s.
  - The Second World War created a need for black workers in factories and towns. The greater number of blacks in towns made the organisation of opposition easier.
- In 1944, the ANC formed a **Youth League**, one of its members was **Nelson Mandela**. During the 1940s, many of these young men became leaders of the ANC.
- In 1952, **Chief Luthuli** became leader of the ANC and began the **Defiance Campaign**. In 1955 a congress of all anti-apartheid groups drew up a **Freedom Charter** setting out their demands. The government hit back in 1956 by arresting 156 people and putting them on trial, the **Treason Trial**. This took five years during which time the ANC was without its leaders.
- Black women, particularly hit by apartheid, also organised protests like the **bus boycotts** against fare increases.

# South Africa (4)

- Some ANC members felt frustrated by non-violent protest methods. In 1959, more militant members split off to set up the **Pan-African Congress**. In **1960**, they held a demonstration at **Sharpeville** which was fired on by police, sixty-nine protesters were killed. There was worldwide protest, but the government merely arrested thousands of people and banned the ANC, SACP and PAC.
- Mandela and some other ANC members decided non-violence had failed, so they formed **Umkhonto we Sizwe** to sabotage property. In 1961, they blew up power lines. Mandela and eight others were arrested. They were prosecuted in the **Rivonia Trials, 1964**, and sentenced to life imprisonment on **Robben Island**. Other ANC leaders fled into exile to seek support or to train as guerrillas.
- There was also resistance from young people. In 1969, the **South African Students' Organisation** was set up by **Steve Biko**, who began the **Black Consciousness Movement**. His activities led to his expulsion from university and, in 1977, to his arrest, torture and death.
- Youth protests continued. The anger of school students at unequal funding for black schools came to a head in **1976**. The government ordered that half of school lessons should be taught in Afrikaans. School students in Soweto organised demonstrations which soon turned into the **Soweto Riots**.

*Police disperse demonstrators in Soweto, 1976*

- Despite police violence, the demonstrations spread all over South Africa. This time, the police found it difficult to re-establish control and many students joined the ANC guerrillas.

## South Africa (1–4)

1 What does 'Boer' mean? (1)

2 What language did the Boers speak? (1)

3 Why did the Great Trek begin? (1)

4 Name *one* of the two independent republics set up by the Boers by 1854. (1)

5 What war led to the Boer republics becoming part of the British Empire's new colony, the Union of South Africa? (1)

6 Name the political party set up by Dr Malan. (1)

7 What does 'apartheid' mean? (1)

8 Why did the Second World War increase demands from whites for more segregationist laws in South Africa? (1)

9 Name *one* of the racial categories set up by the Population Registration Act of 1950. (1)

10 Who became Prime Minister of South Africa in 1958? (1)

11 Give *two* ways in which the government of South Africa created a police state to prevent resistance to apartheid. (2)

12 What were the main black and the main white organisations opposed to apartheid? (2)

13 What ANC resistance campaign began in 1952? (1)

14 Why did Nelson Mandela and some other ANC leaders set up the organisation Umkhonto we Sizwe (Spear of the People) in 1960? (2)

15 Explain the following: the Rivonia Trials; the Black Consciousness Movement; the Soweto Riots. (3)

SCORE

**1** Farmer. (1) Used to describe the early Dutch settlers. Later, they became known as Afrikaners.
**2** Afrikaans. (1)

**3** The Boers resented British rule. (1) In particular, British criticism of their treatment of Africans and the abolition of slavery.
**4** Transvaal *or* Orange Free State (1).

**5** The Boer War, 1899–1902. (1)

**6** (Purified) National Party. (1)

**7** 'Apartness' (1) This meant a much stricter separation between whites and blacks.
**8** Segregation in jobs and housing had been relaxed. (1) More black workers were needed in the towns and factories.
**9** Any *one* from: Black, White, Asian *or* Coloured. (1)

**10** Verwoerd. (1) He was also a member of Broederbond.
**11** Any *two* from: banning orders, detention without trial. police violence *or* BOSS, the Bureau of State Security. (2)
**12** African National Congress. (1) South African Communist Party. (1)

**13** The Defiance Campaign. (1) This was a protest against the pass laws and segregation of public facilities. ANC membership rose to over 100,000.
**14** They felt non-violent protest was ineffective. (1) After the Sharpeville massacre, the ANC was banned. (1)
**15** Mandela and others were sentenced to life imprisonment for sabotage. (1) Started by Steve Biko to increase the self-awareness and confidence of young Blacks. (1) Protests in Soweto townships against: inadequate funding, overcrowding and the use of Afrikaans in schools. (1)

TOTAL

## Apartheid survives, 1960–80

- Internal opposition to apartheid increased from 1960 and South Africa became increasingly isolated from the rest of the world.
- Opposition came from the:
  - **United Nations**
    1962 sanctions imposed; 1974 South Africa expelled
  - **British Commonwealth**
    1961 South Africa left after criticism of apartheid
  - **Organisation for African Unity**
    1969 **Lusaka Manifesto** declared its intention to overthrow apartheid by force, if necessary
  - **Anti-apartheid groups** in Britain and elsewhere.
- Despite this hostility, South Africa prospered. It had:
  - **Minerals** Gold, diamonds and chromium were bought by Britain and the USA. They also invested heavily in South Africa.
  - **Low wages** Foreign companies made large profits by using low-paid black workers. They persuaded their governments not to put sanctions on trade with South Africa.
  - **The Cold War** South Africa was fiercely anti-Communist. Western governments supported South Africa as an ally against its non-white pro-Soviet neighbours who could threaten Western control of minerals and oil-supply routes from the Middle East.
  - **Geography** South Africa was surrounded by friendly countries:
    - the Portuguese colonies of **Angola** and **Mozambique**
    - **Rhodesia** (Zimbabwe) ruled by an illegal, white government from 1965.
    - **South-West Africa** (Namibia) was taken over in 1969 by South Africa, in defiance of the UN.
    - **Botswana** which was poor and dependent on trade with South Africa, although it became independent in 1966.

# South Africa (6)

- During this period, the South African economy prospered. It used its new wealth to become more self-sufficient to beat sanctions.
- The government built up its armed forces and secretly developed nuclear weapons.
- The government censored the media heavily, televison was forbidden until 1976.
- Many whites enjoyed a high and improving standard of living with large salaries, big houses, swimming pools. People from Europe emigrated to enjoy this prosperous lifestyle.
- There were a few educated black Africans, successful black businesses and some skilled black workers, but most black South Africans continued to have a hard and poor life.

*A view of Soweto, a township for black people outside Johannesburg*

- Many were forced out of their homes by the **Group Areas Act** of 1950 into poor areas with few amenities, jobs or transport.
- Most Western governments and businesses were prepared to accept, for economic and political motives, the assurances of Prime Minister **Vorster**, 1966–78, that conditions for blacks would improve.

## The end of apartheid

- During the 1980s there were signs that apartheid was running into problems. The long-term reasons included:
  - **Population** By 1980, blacks made up 76 per cent of the population with whites only 13 per cent. In 1948, it had been 69 per cent to 21 per cent. More blacks were moving into urban areas.
  - **Economy** The restrictions and inequalities of apartheid in education and housing for blacks were making it difficult for foreign businesses to find the staff to expand.
  - **Sanctions** Sanctions in the early 1980s were largely ineffective, particularly as Britian and the USA did not enforce them. But sporting links with other countries were cut, which upset many white South Africans.
  - **End of buffer states** The Portuguese colonies became independent after 1975, and in 1980 Rhodesia gained its independence as Zimbabwe. These new countries opposed apartheid and allowed ANC and PAC guerrillas to train there.
- **P W Botha**, Prime Minister between 1978 and 1989, tried to resist these developments with his policy of '**Total Onslaught, Total Strategy**'. This aimed to strengthen links between the National Party, the Army and big business:
  - **Total Onslaught** involved increasing the size of the South African Army, supporting rebels in Namibia, raiding guerrilla bases and assassinating ANC and PAC leaders, a secret 'dirty war'.
  - **Total Strategy** was a limited programme of reforms to win support from Asians, Coloureds and Blacks. These small-scale reforms failed to satisfy demands for full civil and political rights for all black South Africans.

# South Africa (8)

- The short-term reasons for the collapse of apartheid included:
  - **Black trade unions** used the opportunities of the relaxation of laws to increase membership and launch political strikes.
  - **Black secondary school students** formed strong student organisations and organised protests.
  - **ANC guerrillas** used the ending of Pass Laws to enter South Africa and carry out attacks.
  - the **United Democratic Front** was formed in **1983** as a multi-racial group based on the Freedom Charter.
  - **Exiled ANC leaders**, such as Oliver Tambo, called on their supporters to make South Africa ungovernable.
- From 1984 onwards, grievances erupted into outbreaks of violence in black townships and schools. By 1986, there was a state of emergency across most of the country.
- Police violence, broadcast across the world, led to increased protests. Companies were under pressure to end investment in South Africa.
- Growing unrest and economic problems led more extreme Nationalists, who blamed these problems on Botha's reforms, to form a rival Conservative Party in 1982.
- In 1989 **F W de Klerk** became Prime Minister and immediately announced new, far-reaching reforms.
- In 1990, Nelson Mandela was released and guerrilla warfare ended. De Klerk repealed most of the apartheid laws and talks to draw up a new constitution began in 1991 in CODESA. In spite of this, violence continued. Members of the ANC were impatient for change, and Inkatha, assisted by the South African police, were used to stir up trouble.
- In 1992, whites voted in a referendum for complete change.
- The new constitution was agreed in 1993, and free elections were held in 1994. The ANC won 62 per cent of the votes, and Nelson Mandela became President.

## South Africa (5–8)

**1** Which British Prime Minister warned of a 'wind of change' sweeping through Africa? (1)

**2** Who drew up the Lusaka Manifesto in 1969? (1)

**3** When was South Africa expelled from the UN? (1)

**4** How did the Cold War help South Africa? (1)

**5** Which neighbouring white-ruled African country supported South Africa between 1960 and 1980? (1)

**6** Give *one* reason why poorer white South Africans supported the apartheid laws. (1)

**7** Who was the first black Archbishop of Cape Town? (1)

**8** Which apartheid law of 1950 was increasingly used to remove blacks from land wanted by whites? (1)

**9** Who became Prime Minister of South Africa in 1966, promising to improve conditions for blacks? (1)

**10** How was it clear in 1980 that the policy of confining blacks to rural homelands was not working? (1)

**11** Why were the British and US governments in the early 1980s opposed to economic sanctions against South Africa? (2)

**12** Who was the Prime Minister responsible for a series of reforms between 1978 and 1989 and what was his new policy called? (2)

**13** What multi-racial organisation opposing apartheid was led by Allan Boesak and Winnie Mandela? (1)

**14** What effect did international protests and boycotts in the 1980s have on white South Africans? (2)

**15** Who became Prime Minister of South Africa in 1989, committed to a policy of dismantling apartheid? (1)

**16** What was CODESA, and what was its role in the new constitution of 1993 and the free elections in 1994? (2)

# ANSWERS & TUTORIALS

SCORE

**1** Harold Macmillan. (1)

**2** Organisation for African Unity *or* OAU. (1)

**3** 1974. (1)

**4** Western governments supported its anti-communist stand. *or* They wanted to protect its minerals and the oil route round the Cape from pro-Soviet hands. (1)

**5** Rhodesia. (1)

**6** The laws made them feel superior *or* they protected their jobs and wages from black competition. (1)

**7** Desmond Tutu. (1) The Anglican Church, the Progressive Party and Black Sash organisation were white groups opposed to apartheid.

**8** Group Areas Act. (1)

**9** Vorster. (1)

**10** The majority of blacks lived in towns and cities. (1) By 1980 the figure was nearly 70 per cent, in 1950 it was 50 per cent.

**11** Margaret Thatcher and President Reagan were anti-Communist. (1) They did not want to damage their countries' financial and business interests. (1)

**12** Botha. (1) 'Total Onslaught, Total Strategy'. (1)

**13** United Democratic Front (UDF). (1) The UDF criticised the new constitution for maintaining racial divisions and for excluding blacks.

**14** Barclays Bank, Shell and other big companies pulled out of South Africa, (1) which led to inflation, higher taxes and a shortage of foreign goods. (1)

**15** F W de Klerk. (1)

**16** Convention for a Democratic South Africa. (1) The forum for negotiations for a new constitution and elections. (1)

TOTAL

## The origins of the Cold War

- By the end of the Second World War, European countries such as Britain, France and Germany, which had been powerful before the war, were either economically weakened or in ruins.
- The USA and the USSR were the two dominant **superpowers**.
- They were allies in war, but within a year tensions developed, leading to, what in 1947 was called, a **Cold War**. This Cold War involved:
  - **arms race**
  - **rivalry** in, for example, the space race and sport
  - **propaganda** with each side claiming their system was better
  - **spying**
  - **control** of neighbouring countries
  - **substitute wars** where each side helped their allies fight the other superpower or its allies.
- The Cold War had several long-term causes:
  - The **Soviet Union** feared the West. It had been invaded three times since 1914 through east European countries ruled by right-wing governments. Britain and the USA had helped the Whites in the Civil War. Stalin distrusted the refusal of Britain and France to oppose Hitler between 1936 and 1939, and their delay in invading Western Europe to relieve German pressure on the USSR. The economy was devastated by the Second World War in which over twenty million Russians had died. In 1945, the Soviet Union was the only **Communist** country in the world, it feared the US would attempt to overthrow Communism by using its monopoly of the nuclear bomb.
  - As **capitalists**, the **USA** and **Western European** countries feared Stalin and the Communists wanted to spread revolution across the world. They also feared the end of political freedom and democracy which would reduce opportunities for investment and profits.

## The Cold War begins

The Cold War also had **short-term causes** in the years 1945 to 1948.

- **Yalta Conference, February 1945** Churchill, Roosevelt and Stalin met to negotiate the last stages of the war and the peace.
  - There were vague agreements about the holding of free elections and that Eastern Europe should be a Soviet 'sphere of influence'.
  - The division of control of Germany by the victors was agreed as a temporary measure.
  - The USSR was to take over parts of eastern Poland.

*Churchill, Roosevelt and Stalin at Yalta*

- Roosevelt died in April 1945. His successor **Truman** was much more anti-Communist.
- The Allies next met at the **Potsdam Conference** from July to August **1945**. There were disagreements over the borders of **Poland** and **Germany**.
- Between 1945 and 1948, the Soviet Union extended its control over Eastern European countries. In 1946, Churchill made his famous '**Iron Curtain**' speech to describe the division of Europe into two camps.
- Stalin said the '**satellite**' countries in eastern Europe were only a **buffer zone**. But the USA and West Europe saw Soviet action as part of a plan to take over all of Europe.
- By 1948, both sides in the Cold War feared and distrusted each other.

## The Truman Doctrine, Containment and the Berlin Airlift

- In 1947, Truman announced his **Truman Doctrine**. It was a policy of **containment** to stop the spread of Communism. He set up the National Security Council (NSC) and the Central Intelligence Agency (CIA).
- As part of this policy of containment, Truman decided to give massive economic aid to Western Europe. The **Marshall Plan**, or **Marshall Aid**, as it was known, also helped US industry. By 1952, when the aid ended, the difference in the standard of living between East and West Europe was much greater.
- Cold War tensions were also increased by the **Berlin Crisis**, which began in June 1948.
- The West and the Soviet Union continued to disagree about whether Germany should be made to pay reparations for war damages.
- In 1947, Britain and the US merged their zones and in 1948, France had added theirs. A new currency, the Deutschmark, was introduced to help rebuild the German economy. Stalin was not consulted.
- Stalin, fearing a wealthy and revived Germany, responded with the **Berlin Blockade**. He hoped to force the Allies out of their zones of Berlin, which was in the Soviet sector of the country.
- Truman and the West responded with the **Berlin Airlift**. Ten months later, in May 1949, the Soviet Union later ended the Blockade.
- Germany was divided, the Allies formed their zones into **West Germany**, the Soviet Union later made their zone into **East Germany**.
- The Berlin Crisis deepened mutual distrust and the Iron Curtain became increasingly physical with barbed wire, mines and guard posts separating Eastern and Western Europe.

## Containment around the world: Korea

- The Cold War deepened in **1949** when:
  - the USSR exploded its own atomic bomb, so ending the four-year-old US monopoly of nuclear weapons.
  - China became Communist.
- Anti-Communist hysteria developed in the USA. **McCarthyism**, named after a young senator, meant many people, falsely accused of Communism, lost their jobs.
- In 1950, the National Security Council sent **NSC 68,** to Truman telling him about Communist activities all over the world, and saying his containment policy would have to operate worldwide.
- In June 1950, a crisis developed in **Korea**. Like Germany, Korea had been split at the end of the Second World War into a capitalist south and a communist north, divided by the 38th parallel. After many border clashes, the North invaded the South in an attempt to re-unite the country.
- The US, believing in the **Domino Theory**, decided to use the UN to 'contain' this Communist threat. It was able to do so because the USSR, which could have vetoed the decision, was boycotting the Security Council.
- Most of the troops were American, and the UN force of soldiers from eighteen countries was commanded by US **General MacArthur**. By October, North Korean troops were pushed back beyond the 38th parallel.
- Then, in breach of the UN resolution, MacArthur invaded North Korea, leading his troops near to the Chinese border and ignoring Chinese warnings. China then sent in 200,000 troops, which soon pushed the UN forces back across the 38th parallel.
- There was stalemate from from 1951 to 1953, when the new US President Eisenhower agreed a ceasefire. Korea remained divided.

## The Cold War (1–4)

**1** What is meant by 'Cold War'? (1)

**2** What were the CIA and the KGB? (1)

**3** Which of the two superpowers saw Central and Latin America as its 'sphere of influence'? (1)

**4** At which conference did Churchill, Roosevelt and Stalin re-draw the borders of Poland and allow Greece to be a British 'sphere of influence'? (1)

**5** Give *one* reason why Stalin's fears were increased when Truman became the new US President in April 1945. (1)

**6** Name *one* issue which caused disagreement between the Allies at the Potsdam Conference, 1945. (1)

**7** Why did Stalin insist on having East European countries as a 'buffer-zone'? (1)

**8** Why the USA announce its Truman Doctrine in 1947? (1)

**9** How did the Marshall Plan help US industry? (1)

**10** Give *one* reason why Stalin ordered the closing of all road, rail and canal access to West Berlin in June 1948. (1)

**11** What *two* new countries were established after the end of the Berlin Blockade? (2)

**12** What was McCarthyism? (2)

**13** Why did the USA decide to become involved in the Korean War in 1950? (3)

**14** Explain, briefly: **(a)** The USSR's inability to stop UN intervention in Korea; **(b)** Why China became involved in the Korean War;
**(c)** Why Eisenhower agreed to a ceasefire in 1953. (3)

SCORE

**1** Rivalry between the USA and USSR which stopped short of direct 'hot' or military conflict. (1)

**2** Spy organisations. (1) CIA (USA), KGB (USSR).

**3** USA. (1)

**4** Yalta. (1)

**5** Truman refused to share nuclear weapons technology. (1) *or* Truman was more anti-Communist than Roosevelt. (1)

**6** Any *one* from: Reparations from Germany. (1) Growing Communist power in Poland. (1) Soviet annexation of the Baltic States and parts of Finland and Russia. (1)

**7** To reduce the risk of future invasion. (1) The USSR was invaded three times through East European countries ruled by right-wing governments.

**8** Britain's inability to support Greek monarchists in their civil war against Greek Communists. (1)

**9** Building up the war-damaged economies of Western Europe created better markets for US industries. (1)

**10** Any *one* from: The merger of the Allied zones in Germany. (1) The introduction of a new German currency without consulting the USSR. (1) General fear of a German revival. (1) To force the Allies out of West Berlin, which was in the Soviet zone (1).

**11** Federal Republic of Germany/West Germany (1) Democratic Republic of Germany/East Germany (1)

**12** Anti-Communist hysteria in the USA (1) organised by Senator McCarthy. (1)

**13** Any *three* from: The USSR exploded its own bomb in 1949. (1) China became Communist in 1949. (1) NSC 68 warned of worldwide Communist activities. (1) Communist North Korea invaded capitalist South Korea. (1) The Domino Theory. (1)

**14** **(a)** It was boycotting the Security Council because the US refused China entry to the UN. (1) **(b)** MacArthur took US/UN troops to the Chinese border. (1) **(c)** 1951–53, there was stalemate. (1)

TOTAL

## Containment around the world: The arms race

- One result of the Korean War crisis was the change by the US from the policy of containment based on the Domino Theory to '**Rolling back Communism**' or 'liberating' countries from Communism.

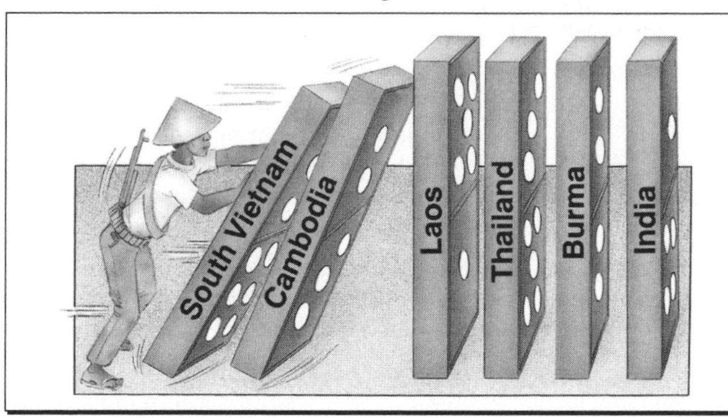


*The Domino Theory*

- This more aggressive idea was particularly associated with **J F Dulles**, the US Secretary of State, 1952–59, and was based on putting pressure on Communist states by:
  - alliances between non-Communist countries
  - more sophisticated and expensive weapons
  - a concerted anti-Communist and pro-West propaganda campaign.
- The USA had formed **NATO** in **1949**, a military alliance in which it was the most powerful member. Under Dulles, the USA created a global system of anti-Communist alliances with **SEATO** and **CENTO**.
- While the West said these were defensive alliances to contain Communism, the Soviet Union and China saw them as aggressive alliances, surrounding them with hostile countries in which the USA had air bases and missile sites.

# THE COLD WAR (6)

- In 1945, the US was the only country with nuclear weapons. It dropped atom bombs on Hiroshima and Nagasaki. Soviet fears, in the growing Cold War, led to an **arms race**. They eventually developed their own nuclear weapons in **1949**.
- As the USA was much wealthier than the Soviet Union, it could better afford this arms race. The US developed the more powerful **hydrogen** bomb which it exploded in **1952**. The USSR produced an H-bomb in **1953**.
- US President Eisenhower decided to build up massive US superiority in the number of nuclear weapons and the number of bombers able to deliver them, based on the theory of **massive retaliation**. So far, each new thrust in the arms race had come from the USA.
- In **1957**, the USSR launched the first satellite ('**sputnik**') into space. This spurred the US to develop **ICBMs**, missiles which delivered nuclear weapons. These began to replace bombers.
- A new arms race was developing. The US was always superior in numbers and in missile sites around the world because of its alliance systems, but under President Kennedy, the US moved to a new policy known as **Mutually Assured Destruction (MAD)**.
- A further twist came in **1960**, when the US developed **submarines** capable of firing nuclear weapons. The USSR soon followed suit.
- In the 1970s, **MIRVs** (Multiple Independent Targeted Re-entry Vehicles) were developed.
- From the 1950s people's opposition to the arms race grew. They objected to the huge loss of life from nuclear weapons, the effects of radiation and the cost of these weapons. In Britain, the Campaign for Nuclear Disarmament (CND) was formed in 1957 and was supported by thousands of people.

## Khrushchev, Kennedy and Cuba

- In 1953, Stalin died. After a power struggle, **Khrushchev** emerged as leader. He wanted to improve living standards for Russians and saw the Cold War and its arms race as too expensive.
- Khrushchev's new policy was called '**peaceful coexistence**'. The intention was to end weapons rivalry and to try to overtake the West in economic development. As part of this, he agreed to withdraw Soviet troops from Austria.
- However, the arms race continued. In **1955**, Khrushchev formed the **Warsaw Pact** with all East European countries as a defence alliance against the threat of NATO.
- In **1956**, at the Twentieth Congress of the Communist Party, Khrushchev attacked Stalin's crimes and began a process of **de-Stalinisation**. This did not extend to allowing East European countries, for example **Hungary** in **1956**, to pull out of the Warsaw Pact.
- Despite Khrushchev's wish for peaceful coexistence and a reduction in Cold War tension, problems continued. In **1960**, the USSR shot down a **U2** US spy-plane which was taking photographs over the USSR. US president **Eisenhower** refused to apologise, which resulted in the break-up of a proposed peace conference in Paris.
- Tension increased further when Kennedy and Khrushchev disagreed over the continued division of Germany. In **1961**, the **Berlin Wall** was built by East Germany, splitting Berlin between its Eastern and Western sectors. It became impossible to cross from one part of the city to the other.

*A clergyman whose parish was cut in two by the Berlin Wall.*

# The Cold War (8)

- The greatest tension between the Soviet Union and the USA came in 1962, with the **Cuban missile crisis**.
- The problem began in **1959**, when **Castro** led a revolution which overthrew Cuba's corrupt and brutal dictator Batista, who had been supported by the US government and businesses.
- US opposition to Castro's policies led him to turn to the USSR for support. In **1961**, the US backed an attempt by Cuban exiles to invade Cuba in the **Bay of Pigs** incident. This failed, and Cuba appealed to the USSR for help. In 1962, US spy-planes noticed missile sites, without missiles, in Cuba.
- Soviet short-range missiles could reach the US from Cuba, so Kennedy ordered US warships to put a **blockade** around Cuba, to prevent delivery of Soviet missiles.

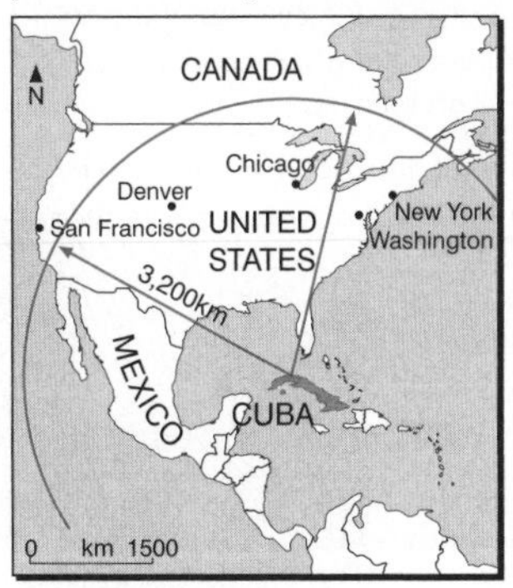


*The Cuban missile crisis*

- After much negotiation, Khrushchev ordered the Soviet ships with the missiles to sail away from Cuba, and a nuclear war was narrowly avoided.
- This crisis led to attempts to improve relations in 1963:
  - the setting up of a **hotline** telephone link between the White House and the Kremlin.
  - a **Test Ban Treaty**.

## The Cold War (5–8)

**1** Explain, briefly, the 'Domino Theory'? (1)

**2** Who was the US official associated with the replacement of 'containment' of Communism by the more aggressive policy of 'rolling back' Communism? (1)

**3** When did the USSR develop its first atom bomb? (1)

**4** What more powerful nuclear weapon did the USA explode in 1952? (1)

**5** What new twist was added to the arms race by the Soviet Union in 1957? (1)

**6** What did Kennedy mean when, in the 1960 presidential elections, he claimed there was a 'missile gap' between the USA and USSR? (1)

**7** What do the initials MIRV stand for? (1)

**8** Who was the Soviet leader associated with the policy of 'peaceful coexistence' between Communism and capitalism? (1)

**9** Why did Hungarians rebel in 1956 and what was the Soviet response? (2)

**10** What was the Warsaw Pact of 1955, and why was it formed? (2)

**11** What was the U2 incident of 1960 and what impact did it have on US–Soviet relations? (2)

**12** Why did Germany build the Berlin Wall? (2)

**13** Why did the Soviet Union attempt to put missile bases on Cuba in 1962? (2)

**14** What did the USA secretly agree to, after the USSR had dismantled its missile sites in Cuba? (2)

SCORE

**1** The belief that Communism was taking over the world country by country. (1) *or* When a country went Communist, its neighbour would soon follow. (1)

**2** J. F. Dulles. (1)

**3** 1949 (1). This ended the nuclear monopoly held by the US since 1945.

**4** Hydrogen or H-Bomb. (1)

**5** Launch of a satellite or 'Sputnik'. (1) This made the delivery of nuclear weapons by missile possible.

**6** The USSR had more ICBMs than the USA. (1) In fact by 1963, the USA had 550, the USSR 100.

**7** Multiple Independent-targeted Re-entry Vehicles. (1)

**8** Khrushchev. (1) He also began a policy of limited de-Stalinisation in the USSR and Eastern Europe.

**9** Continued Soviet control. (1) They sent tanks in to crush it. (1)

**10** A military alliance formed by the Soviet Union and most East European countries. (1) To counter the threat posed by NATO. (1) Also to maintain Soviet control of Eastern Europe.

**11** When the USSR shot down a US spy plane over the USSR. (1) A Paris peace conference broke up. (1)

**12** To stop skilled East Germans fleeing to the more affluent west (1). To make it harder for western spies to enter East Germany.

**13** Any *two* from: Cuba requested protection from US attacks. (1) Short-range missiles on Cuba would balance the USA's long-range missiles. (1) As a bargaining point to remove US missiles from Turkey. (1)

**14** Not to attack Cuba again. (1) To withdraw US missiles from Turkey. (1)

TOTAL

## Vietnam and the end of containment

- Vietnam became another flashpoint in the Cold War. The **Vietminh**, a nationalist army fighting for independence from the French, was led by a Communist, **Ho Chi Minh**. The Communist victory in China in **1949** led the US, because of the Cold War, to support the French.
- After defeat at **Dien Bien Phu** in 1954, the French withdrew. The **Treaty of Geneva** temporarily divided Vietnam into the **North**, ruled by the Communists, and the **South**, ruled by a landlord class.
- A Communist resistance movement, the **Vietcong**, began to attack the undemocratic government in the South. The Vietcong were aided by North Vietnam, which was supported by the USSR. The US sent CIA military 'advisers' and weapons to help the South.
- By 1962, Kennedy had greatly increased US aid. The unpopular government of South Vietnam soon lost control of half the country.
- In 1964, President **Johnson** committed the US to the Vietnam War. Congress passed the **Tonkin Resolution**. In 1965, Johnson escalated the war with **Operation Rolling Thunder**. By 1969, there were 500,000 US troops in Vietnam, but with little success.
  - **Guerrilla warfare** is difficult when your enemy knows the land well and you cannot see them.
  - **US morale** was low, fighting was difficult and many soldiers did not care about the cause for which they were fighting.
  - **US tactics** included extensive bombing, defoliants and napalm. Civilians were affected and many innocent people killed.
  - **Public opinion** in the USA was not supportive, many soldiers were dying, the war was expensive and people were not proud of their country's tactics, for example, the My Lai massacre.
- The **1968 Tet Offensive** made it clear the US could not win. President Nixon began a policy of Vietnamisation and peace negotiations. In **1973** the US withdrew from Vietnam. In **1975** the war finally ended when the North defeated the South.
- US 'containment' policy saw Communists win power in Vietnam, Cambodia and Laos, often with massive popular support.

## Détente

- By the late 1960s, both superpowers wanted a lessening of Cold War tensions and a halt to the arms race, because of the:
  - **huge cost**, especially for the relatively poorer USSR.
  - **increased danger of war**, after the Cuban missile crisis, systems errors, spread of nuclear weapons to other countries.
  - **increased opposition to nuclear weapons**.
- In addition
  - the **USA** wanted to be friendlier with China to prevent its allying with the USSR. It also re-thought its Cold War strategies after the economic and political costs of involvement in Vietnam.
  - the **USSR** wanted friendship with the USA to stop it allying with China.
  - **China** wanted an ally against the USSR and to increase trade with the West.
- This process was called **détente**. Its main supporters were Presidents **Nixon** and **Carter** in the USA, President **Brezhnev** in the USSR and Chairman **Mao Zedong** in China.
- Evidence of détente:
  - **1968 Nuclear Non-Proliferation Treaty**
  - **1971** USA allowed **China** to join the UN
  - **1972** President Nixon visited China, and the **SALT** treaty between the USA and the USSR.
  - **1975 Helsinki Agreement** on 1945 European borders and human rights.
  - **1979 SALT 2** but the treaty was not signed because the USSR sent troops into Afghanistan.
- But the arms race continued and there were verfication problems with the SALT 1. The USA and USSR still tended to support different sides. The USSR often ignored the human rights agreed at Helsinki.
- In **1980**, **Reagan** became US President and detente ended and Cold War attitudes returned so beginning a second Cold War.

## The USSR in Eastern Europe

- In the 1950s, while the main focus of the Cold War was on Korea and Vietnam, Eastern Europe remained under Soviet domination.
- As Europe recovered from the Second World War, many people in East Europe saw they had a **lower standard of living** and **less freedom** than people in West Europe. Such comparisons led to serious protests.
- **Hungary, 1956**
  After Khrushchev's 1956 speech denouncing Stalin's crimes, large demonstrations forced Rakosi, a hardline Stalinist, to resign. He was replaced by **Nagy**. At first, the USSR allowed some reforms, then, fearing Nagy was going to take Hungary out of the Warsaw Pact, Russian tanks were sent in to crush the revolt. Nagy was replaced by **Kadar**, another Communist.
- **Czechoslovakia, 1968**
  Czechoslovakia had been the country with the most developed democracy and economy in East Europe, but by 1968 its economy was stagnant. In 1968, the hardline Stalinist Novotny was replaced by **Dubcek**, a reformist Communist, who wanted '**socialism with a human face**'. This **Prague Spring** was ended by the tanks of the Warsaw Pact forces.
- Brezhnev, the Soviet leader, announced his **Brezhnev Doctrine**:
  - No member of the Warsaw Pact could leave it.
  - No multi-party systems would be tolerated.
- **Poland, 1980**
  Protests in Poland were over economic issues. In 1980, a depression meant demands could not be met. **Lech Walesa** formed **Solidarity**, an independent trade union with mass support. Some of the strikers' demands went against the Brezhnev Doctrine. In **1981**, **General Jaruzelski** became prime minister, Walesa was arrested and Solidarity suspended. In 1986, Solidarity and Walesa began to protest again.

## The end of the Cold War

- Cold War tensions began again in 1980. US President **Reagan**, 1980–88, was very anti-Communist and against détente. He claimed that the US had fallen behind in the arms race. He doubled US arms spending in a new campaign against the USSR. New weapons, like the **neutron bomb**, **Cruise** and **MX**, were developed. **START** talks between the USA and the USSR broke down in 1985.
- In the same year **Gorbachev** became leader of the USSR. He was more anxious to improve living standards and industrial efficiency, and to give greater freedom to Soviet citizens, than to follow the US in a new arms race.
- Because the USSR was less wealthy, it took 25 per cent of national spending to attempt to keep up with US weapons development, which cost the US only 7 per cent of its spending
- Gorbachev realised that to end the arms race, the Cold War must end. In **1986** in **Reykjavik** and in **1987** in **Washington**, he made such major concessions on nuclear weapons that Reagan could only agree. These led to:
  - **1987 INF** (intermetiate Nuclear Force) **Treaty**
  - **1991 START** (Strategic Arms Reduction Treaty).
- Gorbachev ended Soviet involvement in Afghanistan. He made it clear that Soviet troops would no longer be sent into Eastern Europe to prop up undemocratic and unpopular Stalinist rulers.
- From **1989** onwards, the East European satellites soon passed out of Soviet control and in **1990**, **Germany was reunited** and the Berlin Wall was knocked down.
- Gorbachev's policies in the Soviet Union met much opposition from supporters of old-style Soviet leaders. Economic problems and nationalist unrest led to the collapse of the Soviet Union in **1991**.
- So, by 1991, with the end of the Soviet Union, all Eastern European countries independent and moving towards capitalism, and the end of the arms race, the Cold War was clearly over.

## The Cold War (9–12)

1 Who were the Vietcong? (1)

2 What was Operation Rolling Thunder? (1)

3 Explain, briefly, what was meant by 'détente'. (1)

4 Which country was allowed by the US to join the United Nations in 1971? (1)

5 Which US President is associated with the revival of the Cold War in 1980? (1)

6 Which East European country tried to end Soviet domination in 1956? (1)

7 Why did the Soviet Union decide to re-assert its control of this country? (1)

8 Who was the liberal Communist who, in 1968, attempted to introduce 'Socialism with a human face' in Czechoslovakia? (1)

9 What was the 'Brezhnev Doctrine'? (1)

10 What was the name of the independent trade union set up by workers in Poland in 1980? (1)

11 Name the US President who referred to the Soviet Union as the 'evil empire' and the British Prime Minister who supported him in a new arms race. (2)

12 Identify *two* new weapons developed by the US in its new Cold War arms race. (2)

13 Who became the leader of the Soviet Union in 1985, and why did he attempt to end the Cold War? (3)

14 What do the initials INF, START and CIS stand for? (3)

SCORE

**1** Communist guerillas of South Vietnam.

**2** The massive bombing of North Vietnam. (1) President Johnson began this in 1965.

**3** A lessening of Cold War tensions between the superpowers *or* Attempts to halt the arms race. (1)

**4** (Communist) China. (1) This was part of US policy to isolate the Soviet Union.

**5** Reagan. (1) He had supported McCarthy in the 1950s.

**6** Hungary. (1)

**7** Khrushchev feared that Nagy (a liberal Communist) was losing control of the situation. *or* He feared Hungary was about to leave the Warsaw Pact. (1)

**8** Dubcek. (1)

**9** No East European country could leave the Warsaw Pact. *or* No multi-party systems would be tolerated in Eastern Europe. (1) He announced this after Warsaw Pact forces had ended Dubcek's 'Prague Spring' in Czechoslovakia.

**10** Solidarity. (1) It was led by Lech Walesa.

**11** Reagan. (1) Thatcher. (1)

**12** Any *two* from: neutron bomb; Cruise; MX missiles; 'Star Wars' defence system. (2)

**13** Gorbachev. (1) The cost of the arms race was too great (1) and this was causing serious economic problems for the USSR. (1)

**14** Intermediate Nuclear Force. (1) Strategic Arms Reduction Treaty. (1) The INF Treaty 1987 agreed to remove all medium-range missiles from Europe. START, 1991, dealt with long-range missiles. Commonwealth of Independent States (1) Set up when the USSR collapsed in 1991. This, and the end of the arms race and Soviet domination of Eastern Europe, meant the Cold War was over.

TOTAL

## Why was the United Nations started?

- During the Second World War, Allied leaders met several times to discuss how to prevent war in the future. In 1941, Roosevelt and Churchill drew up the **Atlantic Charter**, based on **Four Freedoms**.
- They believed it was lack of these freedoms that caused wars, and decided an international organisation was needed to promote these ideas, and to put pressure on nations ignoring them.
- In **1942**, they drew up the **Declaration of the United Nations**. This attempted to draw lessons from the failure of the League of Nations in the inter-war years 1919–39. The Declaration had six main points.
- Roosevelt was especially keen on the idea of a United Nations Organisation. The idea was discussed at a series of meetings between 1943 and 1945:
  - **1943 Moscow** The USSR and China agreed, with Britain and the US, to support the idea of a United Nations.
  - **1944 Dumbarton Oaks** Discussions on how the UN would work.
  - **1945 Yalta** Britain, USA and USSR agreed to the plans.
- In June **1945** fifty-one countries signed the **Charter of the United Nations** at **San Francisco**. The first meeting of the UN was in London in 1946.
- In 1952, the UN set up a permanent headquarters in **New York**.
- The main part of the UN organisation is the **General Assembly**. Each country, whatever its size, has one vote. All resolutions need a two-thirds majority to succeed.
- In addition, there is the **Security Council**, which has five **Permanent Members** and five other members from other nations for two years at a time. Each of these has the power of **veto**, they can block any decision of the Security Council.

- The Security Council can recommend rapid action:
  - **economic sanctions** against a country acting against the Charter.
  - **military intervention** UN members contribute soldiers to a peacekeeping force, which the League of Nations did not have.
- The head of the UN is the **Secretary-General** who has no loyalty to a country or any other organisation.
- There are also the:
  - **International Court of Justice** based at The Hague in the Netherlands
  - **Social and Economic Council** which co-ordinates the work of the various UN agencies, the most widely-known of which are: **WHO**, **UNICEF**, **UNESCO** and **UNHCR**.

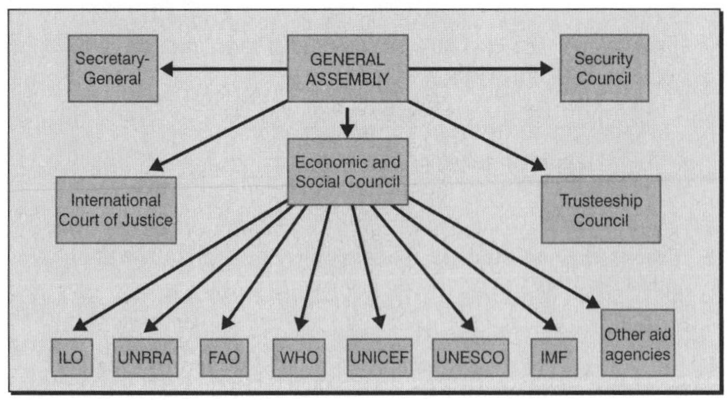


*The structure of the United Nations*

- The main ways in which the UN differs from the League of Nations are:
  - all nations should belong;
  - no country can veto General Assembly resolutions;
  - the Secretary General must act in the interests of peace, not of a few more powerful countries;
  - the UN can use armed force.

## The United Nations from 1945–70

- The hopes of the UN's founders were partially frustrated after 1945 because of the Cold War between the USA and USSR and their allies.
- The USSR felt the UN was dominated by the USA and the West. The USA and its allies had a four-to-one majority in the Security Council, so the USSR frequently used its veto.
- In 1949, the Chinese Communists won their civil war and became the new government of China. The Nationlists retreated to Formosa (Taiwan). The USA refused to allow Communist China to join the UN.
- In **1950**, the General Assembly approved the '**Uniting for Peace**' resolution, so that if an important issue was blocked by the Security Council it could be dealt with by the General Assembly.
- On several occasions UN peacekeeping forces were sent in to keep warring sides apart:
  - **1957–67 Middle East** on the Israel–Egypt border
  - **1964 Cyprus** to keep Greeks and Turks apart
  - **1965 Kashmir** to keep India and Pakistan apart
- On two occasions, the UN sent armed forces to intervene in a crisis:
  - **1950–53 Korean War** For once, the USSR could not use its veto as it was boycotting the Security Council.
  - **1960–64 Congo** Civil War broke out in 1960 after independence. An international force of 20,000 UN soldiers eventually intervened. The UN also supplied medical aid and food.
- The UN was not involved in many of the international crises between 1945 and 1970. This was partly because of the Cold War and the use of the veto in the Security Council by the USSR, and partly because many of the crises were seen as 'internal affairs'.

## How has the United Nations changed since 1970?

- Since 1945, the size of the UN has more than trebled. There are now 184 members of the General Assembly. Most of these new members are African and Asian countries which gained their independence in the 1960s and 1970s.
- The majority of UN members are now **LDCs** ('Less Developed Countries') so the economic, health and educational agencies of the UN have become more important. The General Assembly often criticises the economic policies of the richer nations.
- Several of these richer nations who set up the UN and paid most of its costs now pay little attention to the UN.
- The new membership has also questioned the role of the countries that are on the Security Council:
  - Are the five permanent nations now the most important?
  - What about Germany and Japan?
  - Why is no African country represented as permanent member?
- The cost of running the UN has led some richer countries like the USA and Britain to leave agencies such as UNESCO. The US has regularly refused to pay part of its UN contributions.
- During the Cold War, the UN took little part in international affairs. Wars in the **Middle East**, **Afghanistan**, **the Falklands** and **Iran–Iraq** were all dealt with outside the UN.
- When the Cold War ended, the UN was used to intervene in crises:
  - **Gulf War, 1991** As in Korea, most of the forces were American.
  - **Yugoslavia, 1991** A peacekeeping force between Serbs and Bosnians, though UN intervention had little effect.

## The United Nations (1–4)

1. Name *one* of the two Allied leaders who drew up the Atlantic Charter in 1941. (1)
2. Give *one* of the 'Four Freedoms' they believed was necessary to avoid war in the future. (1)
3. At which conference, in February 1945, did Stalin agree to US and British plans for a United Nations? (1)
4. Where were permanent headquarters for the UN set up in 1952? (1)
5. What power, which the League of Nations lacked, does the UN have to solve international crises? (1)
6. What colour are the helmets worn by soldiers of UN peacekeeping forces? (1)
7. Name *one* of the five original permanent members of the Security Council. (1)
8. What does 'veto' mean? (1)
9. What was the 'Uniting for Peace' resolution adopted by the UN's General Assembly in 1950? (1)
10. Who is the present Secretary-General of the UN? (1)
11. Why did the Soviet Union not block the Security Council's decision in 1950 to send forces to help South Korea against North Korea? (2)
12. What African country asked for UN help in 1960 when civil war broke out? Who was its Prime Minister? (2)
13. What were the *two* occasions in the 1950s and 1960s when UN forces kept warring sides apart? (2)
14. Why did the UN not intervene in the Berlin Airlift, the Suez Crisis, the Hungarian Revolution, the Cuban missile crisis or the Vietnam War? (2)
15. Name *two* major crises of the 1990s which have seen UN involvement. (2)

SCORE

**1** Roosevelt *or* Churchill. (1)
**2** Freedom from want; freedom of speech; freedom from fear; freedom of religion. (1)

**3** Yalta. (1)

**4** New York. (1)

**5** Use of a UN military force. (1) Soldiers from the army of any UN member can be sent to try to keep the peace in areas of conflict.
**6** Light blue. (1)

**7** USA *or* USSR *or* Britain *or* France *or* (Nationalist) China. (1)

**8** The power to block any decision. (1) Just one Security Council member can prevent any UN action by voting against it.
**9** This decided that if any important issue was vetoed in the Security Council, it could be dealt with by the General Assembly. (1)

**10** Kofi Annan. (1) He is from Ghana and took office in 1997.
**11** It was boycotting the Security Council (1) because the US refused Communist China entry into the UN. (1)

**12** Congo. (1) Lumumba. (1) At first the UN refused, so Lumumba went to the USSR. Some Western countries backed the other side, so the UN acted.
**13** Any *two* from: the Israeli–Egyptian border, 1957–67. (1) Cyprus, 1964. (1) Kashmir, 1965. (1)
**14** The Cold War and the frequent use of the veto in the Security Council. (1) Many crises were seen as 'internal affairs'. (1)

**15** The Gulf War, 1991. (1) Yugoslavia, 1991. (1) The collapse of the USSR and the end of the Cold War has made it easier for the UN to make decisions.

TOTAL

# Score Chart (1)

| Topic | *Check yourself* | Points out of 20 |
|---|---|---|
| The First World War (1–4) | 1 | |
| The First World War (5–8) | 2 | |
| The Peace Treaties (1–6) | 3 | |
| Germany, 1918–1945 (1–4) | 4 | |
| Germany, 1918–1945 (5–6) | 5 | |
| Germany, 1918–1945 (7–10) | 6 | |
| The Russian Revolution (1–4) | 7 | |
| The Russian Revolution (5–8) | 8 | |
| Stalin and Russia (1–4) | 9 | |
| Stalin and Russia (5–8) | 10 | |
| The USA, 1919–1941 (1–4) | 11 | |
| The USA, 1919–1941(5–8) | 12 | |
| International Relations (1–4) | 13 | |
| International Relations (5–8) | 14 | |
| South Africa (1–4) | 15 | |
| South Africa (5–8) | 16 | |
| The Cold War (1–4) | 17 | |
| The Cold War (5–8) | 18 | |
| The Cold War (9–12) | 19 | |
| The United Nations (1–4) | 20 | |

# Score chart (2)

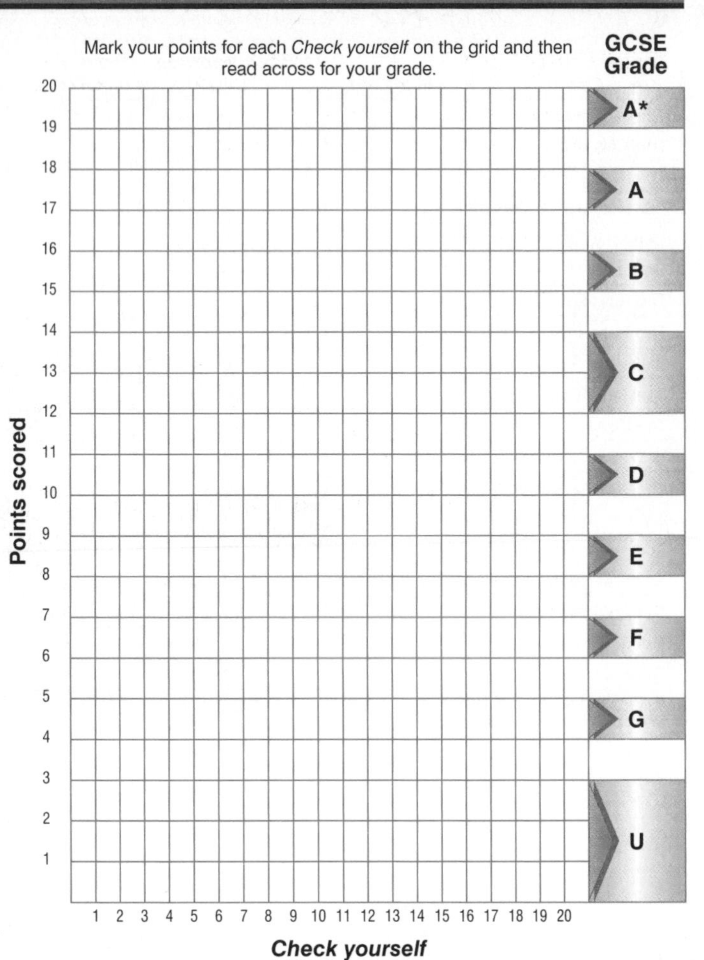